Freedom through Numbers

by Finding Your "I AM"

A New Take on Numerology

Darlene Chadbourne

Copyright © 2020 by Darlene Chadbourne.

All rights reserved. No part of this publication may be copied, reproduced, stored in a retrieval system, or transmitted in any form or by any means, electronic, mechanical, recording or otherwise, without the prior written permission of the author.

ISBN #978-0-578-67479-7

Graphics designed by Nicole Foster Hadley

I would like to dedicate this book
to all the human angels in my life
who have continued to encourage me
to write this book.

Table of Contents

Foreword 11
   Every Word I Speak 13
Preface 15
   The Magic of 50 15
   Don't Tie Me Down 20
      The Tunnel 23
   Finding Your Life 30
      Stranger to Myself 32
      Cold Pot Belly 33
Part One 35
   Introduction: Numbers and Numerology 35
      Quality vs. Quantity 35
Chapter 1 37
   The Beginning of Numerology for Me 37
   Numerology and Self-Discovery 41
   Vibration of Numbers 43
   Freedom 45
Chapter 2 49
   Native Path Method: Worksheet, Chart, and Blueprint 49

The Blueprint	50
Working the Calculations	53
Letter-to-Number Conversion Chart	54
Worksheet Calculations for your Blueprint	66
Figuring Your Numbers	69
Discovering Your Numbers	73
Calculations for Your Blueprint	81
After the Blueprint	82
Chapter 3	**85**
The Meanings of the Numbers	85
Single Digits 1-9	87
Being an Overdone Number	101
Mastery	105
Master Numbers 11-99	108
An Overdone Master Number	121
Chapter 4	**125**
Working your Numbers, Timing is Everything	125
Temporary Numbers and Timing	126
The Decades	128
What Decade Were You Born In?	129
What Decade is Your Age in Now?	131

Chapter 5 133
- Name Changes 133
- Legal Name Change as an Adult 133
- Name Change through Marriage 134
- Name Change for Adoptions 134

Chapter 6 135
- Adoption 135
- Double Blueprints 135
- Roots and Adoption 136
- The Importance of Roots 138
- Roots and Location 140

Part Two 141

Chapter 7 141
- Finding Your "I AM" 141
- Manifesting: Name It, Claim It, Become It 149
- Defining the "I AM" 150
- The Power of Thoughts and Words 153
- The Power of the "I AM" 154
- Figure 8 "I AM" Exercise 156

Chapter 8 161
- Be the Star that You Are: 161

If You Can't Hide It, Feature It 161

Turn on Your Light for the World to See 165

Chapter 9 169

Affirmations, Working Your Numbers 169

The Poison of Criticism 172

The Power of Words 173

Steps for Creating Affirmations 176

Conclusion 181

Tools 185

Tool #1—Journaling 185

Tool #2—Meditation 185

Tool #4—Releasing Karmic Connections 187

Tool #5—Apply Shape and Form to your numbers and your "I AM" presence. 188

Tool #6—Mind-Mapping 188

Appendix 1: Meaning or Qualities of the Numbers (quick reference) 189

Appendix 2: Blueprint 193

Appendix 3: Star Templates 194

Appendix 4: Word Lists for Creating Affirmations 196

Suggested Reading List 206

Acknowledgements 207

Foreword

The long journey to her enlightenment speaks to the soul of this woman. Darlene Chadbourne shares not only her life journey but the wisdom she has gained through the sacred universal language of numbers. In this book, through her simple instructions, you will discover your "I AM". She guides you on this path to "know thyself", the ancient message inscribed over the portal of the Temple of Apollo at Delphi, a repeated aphorism that arose from ancient Egypt. You will be delighted in the capable hands of this special woman.

Dusty Bunker, 2020

Darlene Chadbourne
~ 12 ~

Every Word I Speak

Every word I speak, every breath I breathe,

every step I take matters to someone;

not everyone, but to someone.

And most of all it matters to me,

that I am participating and doing my part,

for this is what feeds my heart and soul,

and fulfills my mission, my passion, my purpose.

No word, breath, step, mission, passion, or purpose

is too small or too large;

it just is.

Darlene, Sept, 2000

Freedom Through Numbers

Darlene Chadbourne
~ 14 ~

Preface

My purpose in writing this book is to facilitate your personal process in:

- Birthing your complete "I AM" presence;
- Building your self-confident "I AM";
- Becoming your total "I AM".

The Magic of 50

I turned 50 and I knew what I had to do. I knew that this was my chance to make a statement, have a want and speak it out loud. I wanted to know who I was and where I stood and what I thought, and what I felt. No more running on auto-pilot. I wanted to stop, get off the *merry-go-round* and use my mind in an applied and inquisitive manner. I wanted to do a calculated search for the missing piece of me, that I had left who knows where.

I didn't know the *who, how, what, where,* or *when*, but once I stated the want out loud the world at large stepped up to the plate. As long as I showed up to receive, the pieces always came in perfect timing, Not a minute too soon or a minute too late, but at the exact moment I was in a place to notice and receive the answer to my curiosity.

Back in 1993 when I turned 50 my want was to go to college. I didn't need reasons—I knew I had to go.

I was approaching my 50th birthday when my husband and I sold the auto parts store that I managed; one of the three businesses we owned and operated together. The businesses were located next to our home so we could be close by for our children. At this point, three of our four children were well on their way to becoming independent adults, not needing me as much as they did when they were younger.

Thinking about this, I came to the realization that I had lived my life caretaking others. I think I was born an adult, always trying to take care of my mother. She had abandoned me, leaving me with my aunt right after birth. This began my pattern of pleasing people so I would never be abandoned again. At 50, as I was reviewing my identity, I could see myself as a daughter, a loving people-pleasing wife, a mother of four, a business owner, and a very hard worker who was always juggling things to keep everyone happy.

This is when I declared to my mother, husband, and children, "I have spent the first 50 years of my life as a daughter, a wife, a mother and with a full time job. The last 50 years are mine! I am going to college." Attending college was something I had wanted to do ever since I graduated high school, but at that time I was told, "You can't go to college. You have to go to work and contribute to the household expenses." It took me 50 years to break that old pattern and begin doing what I knew I wanted to do.

Darlene Chadbourne

I wanted to open up my gifts and talents, passion and purpose, and mission in this lifetime. The part of me that lay dormant as I tried to people-please others was given a new freedom. When I declared "independence" it was the first time in my life that I named a need, a want and a desire of my own, something that didn't involve putting others' needs first.

The college I chose required that I stay in residence for ten days to plan my study for that semester. Going to campus and having a room of my own brought about an interesting feeling of being totally alone –- and in silence, but not abandoned. I realized in that moment that I had never been anywhere overnight by myself. I had always been with a parent, a husband, or a child, but never alone.

The magic that happened in those ten days was the discovery of a single dim ember of light or energy in my being. It was my spirit. With the encouragement of advisors and other students I was able to uncover the spirit buried so deep within, it turned into a warm glowing ember – a connection I had not experienced before. My spirit was rescued from the piles of ashes that had built up from my energy being used only for others. As I recalled this time with a friend, she remembered, "Your ember burst into flames—I know—I was there, feeling the warmth."

From that point on I have adopted the term *midlife spirit* to identify and honor the person that I discovered and am to this day. I use Midlife Spirit for my email identity for Darlene Chadbourne, owner of a business that I love and am passionate about.

When I gave myself permission to be alone and do what I wanted to do during my four years of college, I discovered that, yes, I am a wife and a mother, but those are not my identities. My identity is that of a free midlife spirit, a numerologist, mentoring people of all ages to find their passion, purpose, and potential.

Turning 50 and going to college opened the door to writing that had been closed long ago. Writing was a tool I used for identifying the lost or hidden parts of my deeply buried original self. The professors said, "Follow your Passion and Trust the Process." I had my doubts that this phrase could accomplish what I needed to get done in the next 6 months. I had no clue what my passion was. Where would I start? In a brainstorming session a professor mentioned the subject of mother/daughter relations. That grabbed my attention. I had a mother and I was a daughter; I am a mother and I have a daughter. I left campus with a list of 20 books on mother/daughter relationships, which led to delving into the psychology of this relationship. As I researched, I found that I was not alone in my issues with my mother and abandonment. The writing brought up deep emotions around the subject.

Well, let me tell you the power of the written word kicked in at full force when I decided to go to college at age 50. The written word freed me enough to create change. Big changes followed.

Darlene Chadbourne

Somewhere between then and now I knew I had to write a book, and I talked about it for years. Then people started to tell me I should write a book. In 2016 I took the leap to show up at a writer's retreat and it was there the project really started. After the second writer's retreat I knew what I had to do. Finish the Book.

Don't Tie Me Down

As I delved into numerology I discovered the magic of 50, which created freedom and change that began my life as a numerologist.

Midlife starts at age 35 and goes to 65, the midway point is age 50. Do you notice each of those ages has a 5 in them? When you are at the mid-point of 50 there is or should be a shifting of gears to empower the rest of your life. 5 is the number of change.

5 is about being a free spirit and finding out what gives you that freedom. It is also about the power of the written word and languages. Change also happens under a temporary vibration of 5.

0 in Numerology means *nothing* and *everything*. 0 is energy from above that uplifts the number it is with to a higher vibration, amplifying the God, Spirit, or Universe's multiplying effect.

The magic of 50, that adds a 0 to the 5, opens the door to the uplifting enlightenment of spiritual input. Spirit talks to us in bits and blurbs, not paragraphs and sentences. So when you put out a want you also need to be ready to receive the answer in whatever form it is delivered.

The more I wrote about my personal experiences the freer I felt. I also learned that these mother/daughter issues are very much a product of the disempowerment of

Darlene Chadbourne

women in our patriarchal society. My reading and writing was bringing my focus to a world much larger than my own personal life.

My presentation for that first semester was titled, *The Tunnel*. Thinking that I had processed all of the emotion, I started to present to the group and my professor. The waterfall of tears began. I then realized that I had not voiced this story out loud for others to hear. Remember, I was the well-put-together, calm people-pleaser when I was in the presence of others.

To my surprise when I finished my professor told me, "…that was a very heartfelt piece of well written poetic prose." Not in my wildest dreams did I think that my passion was connected to my emotions. It was at this point that the writer was born through the power of words fueled by emotion. Writing left me with a sense of freedom through the quality of the number 5.

There are many personal writings that I have inserted throughout the book as chapter dividers. I hope the following essay will help you to see the process that I used to identify and step into my freedom by peeling the layers of emotions and claiming the power in my "I AM" presence.

The Tunnel

I began this journey six months ago as a fifty-one year old who wanted to go to college more than anything else. It seems fitting that I chose Mother/Daughter Relations as my study, since it was my mother who prevented me from entering college right after high school.

Mother/Daughter Relations seemed like a safe enough subject. After all, I am a mother and a daughter. I also have a mother and a daughter, which in my mind was enough qualifications.

I expected to learn more about these relationships and broaden my resources to help my clients free themselves from the co-dependent relationships that were similar to my own. I also wanted to be able to offer a Mother/Daughter Workshop as a finished product. Looking back in hindsight at the person who had these expectations, I see a middle-aged woman with a very narrow focus of a goal to help others with something she could not accomplish herself. She was a person with tunnel vision and very limited ideas.

As I started to read the material for my study, twenty-two books in all, I felt like the little boy who tried to put his thumb in the dike to save the town. I felt like a little girl again with all these emotions held back behind a dam. Never in my wildest dreams did I think that I had so many pent-up emotions. Thankfully I had a good mix of books that enabled me to balance this emotional ride that I was about to encounter.

With the first two books about family systems and family history, I charted what I knew of my family history. I discovered many repetitive patterns showing up throughout the generations. Then there were the books about the history of patriarchy and how it has affected women for centuries. These were the matter-of-fact books that I read as background to diffuse the emotional triggers of this study. The rest of the books are the emotionally charged majority.

As I read more books, there were more powerful emotional triggers. They helped me to really get in touch with the hurt, sad, and empty feelings. Then there were those that allowed me to identify, label, and understand how I got to this point in my life.

Cutting the Ties that Bind, by Phyllis Krystal was a gift that supplied me with the tools to empower me to make changes. These changes were not minor either. Finally, I drew my study to a close, which set the mood for me to sit and contemplate where I have been, what I have done, and where I am today.

This reflection of my first semester would not be complete without my sharing some of my feelings, after all that is what this study was all about:

I suspect that I came into this life as an unwanted baby, who was entering a family who shut off their feelings and denied that feelings even existed. I feel like I have spent the first half of my life in a tunnel with a dam built in front of the entrance, after I entered this world. The dam was to ensure that the feelings and emotions could not flood into the tunnel, making the tunnel a safe place to be. How was I to know anything other than the life in the dark tunnel? That is all my mother and father modeled for me.

I believe they went underground right after my conception. They moved into the dark silence of the underground tunnel because of guilt and disgrace that I believe came from their family and the Catholic Church. Living in the tunnel in darkness and silence with nothing flowing through was very depressing and mundane. Not having anything other to compare my life with at that time, allowed me to believe that this was the way everyone's life was. It was all I knew. With the feelings and emotions dammed off life was very dry.

One day there was a glimmer of hope that came, entering my head from somewhere, saying, "I am tired of going on in this dark tunnel stuck with all of my family in this nothingness place. I wish there was another route that I could take to change my life, to allow me a choice, to allow me to separate from my family and the darkness, to allow me to see what else there is to life." Oh, the power of a thought-form, I never knew it could do so much.

The next day there was a split in the tunnel that offered me the opportunity to make a choice. My families values said—"Stay with us, you don't know what is down that path. This is the well-traveled path. It is the path that has been used for generations before us. It is best to stay the same. We know what is here. Besides there is water on the other path. It is damp and muddy. Someone must have let some feelings escape. Feelings will only get you in trouble. Please don't change. Stay on the same course with us."

This was my glimmer of hope, my thought-form coming to life. It was a change. It was the change I had hoped for, wished for. I cannot pass this up. I have been on dry ground for too long. "Dear family, you have the choice of coming with me into the tunnel of change. I cannot make that choice for you and you cannot make my choice for me." I chose the different path, the path of change.

This is not an easy path, but it is better than the old constant path of repeated steps, over and over without deviation. At first it was muddy and thick and hard to move. It was hard work to pick up one foot and put it in front of the other without getting mired in the guck. Then I really got mired on page 10 of the book *The Circle of Stones* in the discovery of never being wanted and always being held accountable for my grandmother's death. Duerk writes:

"The mother, first representative of the Self to the infant, constellates in the infant what will become the sense of Self within as the child grows." (The Circle of Stones, Duerk, p. 10)

Duerk goes on to explain that if the child doesn't have the mirror of a loving mother, she may grow up without a sense of self, and may never feel worthy. As an

Darlene Chadbourne

adult, the child may feel she has no idea who she is, and may feel abandoned and isolated, as if life is a void.

Losing this mother love equals a loss of safety and security. Comfort, nurturing, and joy may be missing from the experience of life. The child, and consequently the adult, may feel tainted, shamed, and guilty, unworthy of any kind of love. She may also fear that she will never be known for who she truly is deep inside.

I did not lose my mother in body, but I did lose my mother emotionally when:

- she went underground with her feelings
- she passed out at her mother's funeral
- she took on the guilt
- she passed it on to me
- she chose not to deal with her grief
- she didn't want to look at me
- she was ashamed of me
- she gave me to my aunt.

My mother did not look at me. How could she mirror anything, except guilt or nothingness? What is better: the guilt or the nothingness? I suspect she was feeling, "I sinned so God took my mother" when she found out she was pregnant and her mother died shortly after that.

After I cried enough tears and allowed the emotion to flow, it moistened and loosened my mired feet in the tunnel. I not only could move but I could also see a pinpoint of light. Never having seen light before I did not know what it was but I was drawn toward it. I can move along faster now—the mud is lighter and has more moisture and feelings are flowing. It wasn't very long at all before I felt like dancing through the mud. It is *The Dance of Deception*, a dance around unspoken lies and family secrets. Like the time my cousin innocently sent me a picture of my father as a young man. He was not alone in the picture. She made a notation at the bottom of the copy. "This is your father and his first wife, who he was married to for fifteen years." I was devastated because this was news to me. I never knew that he was married to anyone but my mother. This brought a flood of tears enough so I could swim if I wanted. Then I learned to float and let the river of tears take me where ever it flowed. I really did not care where I would end up at this point. The water flowed slowly and freely all by itself without my control so I had a chance to rest.

When I had rested enough. I decided to look where I was and to my surprise, I could see a much larger circle of light and it was expanding quite rapidly. Could this be light, a light at the end of the tunnel? Can I actually begin to see, to see through the tunnel, to see the end of the tunnel?

Now I began to get excited and I am still feeling lighter. With more light shining into the tunnel I began to see something on the walls of the tunnel. There are stories,

Darlene Chadbourne

stories of other motherless daughters and how they found their way out of the black emptiness into the light to see who they were and to find their sense of Self.

Who is this Self, who is jumping for joy to see the light? To experience the expansiveness? To see with unlimited vision and no blinders? As I sit, to take in the view of this beautiful world that is mine to behold, I think of Judith Duerk's book, *I Sit Listening to the Wind*. Her words match my own experience of life.

How many people live in fear of doing something wrong and feeling so judged that we must latch onto any authority who gives us even a crumb of approval? But the risk is that then we never turn inward to learn the truth of who we are.

It takes tremendous courage to look within, and find our guidance for living there, instead of relying on "social norms" or "the mind of the herd" to make decisions about our lives.

At this point, I realize this is the beginning of my journey to self-awareness. I also realize the importance and value of asking questions and not taking everything for granted, even from your *mother*. The research I have encountered, to find the answers to the questions, is the most enjoyable part of my journey. The self-worth that I am beginning to feel as I find out who I am is the biggest reward of all.

Finding Your Life

"The presence of life sustains life."
Henry Beston, *The Outermost House*

It is so important to get to know your life. Your personal life is the life you want to know best. The more you know of yourself the more you can sustain the quality of life you deserve.

Retreats from everyday interaction, from focusing on others, is a gift like no other. It is a gift to yourself to find the silence within that silence. Jewels of thought have been tumbling within, being polished while they wait patiently for you to find a moment or more of silence, so they can make their presence known.

Writing is the most powerful tool for allowing this parade of jewels to enter the runway of paper to be viewed and admired with the *ooh's* and *ahh's* of recognition of extreme value. What was once a simple thought, allowed to tumble for a time, can become the jewel that makes you always wonder, Did I write that?

Once you know yourself, you feel ready for anything that may arise. With your necklace of jeweled amulets, lying beautifully around your neck, you are so ready to present yourself to the world.

Darlene Chadbourne
~ 30 ~

I strongly suggest you keep a daily entry journal, notating all of the unusual signs and clues that spirit leaves for you on a daily basis. It could be a message on the radio or a license plate, a word or phrase, a line in a song or something someone says to you, or even something you overhear in someone else's conversation. I usually perk up if I hear it two times in a short period of time, but if I hear or see it three times or more, I feel it is time to take action.

Stranger to Myself

The door closed long ago never to open,
'til understanding and trust arrived with compassion.

An open door reveals safety encompassing my being,
guarding its precious energy from intrusion or invasion.

I am more of a stranger to myself
than to anyone else I have yet to meet.

Darlene, 2000

Darlene Chadbourne
~ 32 ~

Cold Pot Belly

While searching blindly through
The deep dark depths of my being,
A passer-by peeked in
And caught a slight glimpse of smoldering ash.
The breath of
Patience and gentleness
Fanned the ash
to get it to ignite.
That passer-by was the only one who noticed
The smoldering ash become a spark.
I was too blinded by business then
To bother with ashes.
The air of freedom and encouragement
Were added to the spark,
Which grew to a flame on
The kindling of praise.
Now I am completely engulfed by
The expansion of
The glow, the warmth.
Darlene, 1996

Darlene Chadbourne

Part One
Introduction: Numbers and Numerology

Quality vs. Quantity

Numbers are the language, or the fabric, of the universe, and are used to count and quantify in the material world. Numerology gives attention to the quality of the numbers and the archetypal energies that they hold.

In ancient philosophies, numerology, like astrology, was studied and valued as a tool for individual development and self-understanding. Numerology is a practice, or body of knowledge. It is a tool that is available to help you discover all the nuances of your individual qualities, in the depth and complex nature of who you are. Your individual numbers are attuned to universal frequencies. These frequencies were referred to as the "Music of the Spheres" by Pythagoras, an ancient philosopher and spiritual guru of his time. These frequencies in turn allow you to tune in and align with the part of you that shines, like the brightest star. By knowing your numbers, and working your numbers, you will align with and tune into the universal frequencies.

- Numbers are the language of the universe.
- Numbers take on shape and form through geometry.

You might say the universe operates by a geometric energy code that is all about the numbers relating to shape and form.

- Geometry takes numbers from 2 dimensions to 3 dimensions and beyond.
- Geometry is numbers coming alive through shape, form, and dimension.
- Geometry can animate a number into a material form.

Chapter 1

The Beginning of Numerology for Me

I would have to say I didn't find numerology—it found me. But I didn't start using it at that time.

I was really mired in the numbness and overwhelming feelings that mothers, wives, and business owners experience from time to time. Back in the nineties, I had a psychic reading and the psychic said, "*They* are telling me that you need this book." She handed me *Numerology and the Divine Triangle*, by Faith Javane and Dusty Bunker. '*They*' referred to the guides she was listening to from another realm. As you can see, there is not just Numerology involved here, but also Sacred Geometry, as in the Divine Triangle, referred to in the title.

I brought the book home and read it periodically, as I had a chance, but my household was always quite chaotic.

The universe, or spirit, really wanted me to pay attention to this book. You never know where or how the answers are going to come when you ask the question. "What am I supposed to be doing with my life?"

I used the book to figure out my numbers and my family's numbers, and then it found its way to the bookshelf and sat dormant for many years. Like so many beginners on the spiritual journey, I didn't know what to do with the information the book gave me, or how to put it to practical use. So I developed a system called the *Native Paths Method,* which I will share with you in Chapter 2.

The best thing I ever did for myself was to say, "It's my turn to live my life now." College was the best four years of learning and therapy I ever had because I found out who I was while learning an expanded view of the world that lies beyond my everyday life. There was a person in me that was not a daughter, not a wife, and not a mother, but an individual person. Someone who could stand in the world and do her own thing. Someone who had a brain and a heart. There was someone in there who had emotions, drives, and passions to follow, curiosities to satisfy, and interests that were unique to me. The first five semesters were all about excavating that person by peeling off the layers of the onion to get to the strong core. All this while getting the best education for me.

It was in the sixth semester that I found the golden nugget. It came to me through a professor who said, "You may want to borrow this out-of-print book, *Time Stands Still* for your study this semester." I was very careful with this book, knowing that, unlike the psychic's book, I could not replace it if anything happened to it.

Another series of synchronistic events happened around this same time, laying out the current path that I am traveling. Sacred geometry, labyrinths and numbers all formed patterns and symbols that I could not ignore. The universe, or spirit, kept making the path clearer and clearer. Like many people, it came to me when I was not looking for it. I became a Numerologist, helping people to connect the dots of their own life. Teaching them how to make the connections to the gifts and talents that they already have. Perhaps more importantly, to notice what comes to you in a synchronistic fashion when you are not looking for anything in particular.

My intrigue is the same now as it was when I would get a new connect-the-dot book as a little kid. It comes from the fascination of counting and following the numbers, connecting them together to reveal a picture.

With numerology, I use a client's personal numbers and connect them together to create a picture of not only who that person is, but who that person can be and all the possibilities that are available to them. Some clients can really relate to the picture revealed. Others discover the possibilities that they only allowed themselves to dream about, but never thought those possibilities were theirs for the taking. Still others were opened to possibilities they'd never even imagined possible, yet all they had to do was name it, claim it, and then become it.

Some are searching for help while not knowing what they are looking for, simply knowing there must be more to life for them. Some have been in different kinds of therapies, without knowing what kind of help they are looking for. Some are searching for what more is available to them. Others come because I helped someone else they know. While still others, are following their own inner guidance system after having a chance encounter with someone who mentioned my name. One person recently came because she had overheard a conversation while she was in a store.

Some people are very energy-sensitive and I teach them specific, simple tools to protect their inner core—so they can be more comfortable interacting with others on a day-to-day basis. Some people have been limited by past conditioning, so I teach them how to unlock the doors and take down the limitations so they can feel comfortable letting their inner light shine, radiating like a beacon for others.

Numerology highlights the depth of who we are and gives us permission to follow our passion, center in our true self and have the courage to walk the path we are meant to walk in this lifetime. For some of us it is a step-by-step process; for others it is a one-time visit that validates what they knew all along, and encourages them to follow through on it.

Darlene Chadbourne

Numerology and Self-Discovery

Numerology takes your personal information and carves it down to the core of who you are and who you have the potential to be, which may be very different from who or what you believe you are.

It is an important distinction that numerology is not about the numbers it is instead about your relationship to the numbers and what they say to you about your life and the subject at hand.

There is also an intuitive component to numerology. There is an unseen or unspoken kind of communication that happens when I meet with my client after calculating their numerology blueprint. During this meeting there is a channel that opens. The old adage, "when two or more are gathered for the highest good of all" applies here. Sometimes it is a word or a phrase and at other times it is a question that forms in my mind that I wasn't thinking about, and in fact, has no meaning to me. Yet, when I mention it to the client it almost always opens a door to a deeper dimension of discussion or allows us to make more correlations to the situation we were discussing.

Your name is the essence of who you are. When it is spoken, your name stimulates your inner potential, the reason for your being. Think of graduation day when you hear your full name announced; they are sounding out and honoring your full, complete self in all of its glory. It may or may not feel different, but if you are really listening, you can hear it sounding out your full potential, your full and unique energy vibration, announcing that you are one step closer to fulfilling your full potential and destiny. The sound of hearing your name also connects you to your numbers.

You came into the world on the wings of an energy vibration with the intention to accomplish a mission. Numerology helps you to decode, demystify, and interpret your mission and soul song.

You did not come into this body and this physical plane to help yourself through life. You came into a specific family. You were invited in by an energy vibration of passion to help enhance the life of others, whether you realize it or not. Some families resist the lessons and gifts that their children are called to bring into their families. Others enhance and support the mission you are here for and welcome them with open arms.

Numerology identifies a person's strengths and weaknesses on the spiritual, emotional, mental, and physical planes of existence. Numerology highlights our unique and individual gifts that might lie dormant because of this culture's preferred attention paid to *quantity* over *quality*. How can we reverse this trend of *quantity* over *quality*, to *quality* over *quantity*? Quantity is only one side of the equation to do with numbers—it is necessary but overrated and out of balance. When the *quality* side of numbers or the character traits and morals or spiritual side of numbers is put aside and left out of most of life's equations, our use of numbers is out of balance.

Darlene Chadbourne

Vibration of Numbers

Numerology gives attention to the quality and vibration of numbers and the energies that they hold. Words and names each vibrate to a frequency. When we translate our names into numbers, we discover what our specific frequencies are. Designated by our date of birth and our name, our personal numbers help us to be aware of and balance our full palette of traits and tendencies, the same way an artist does when they use their palette of colors, full of vibrant qualities, to create a balance of shades and hues resulting in either a harmonious or discordant visual delight. We can have that balance, too.

Numerology helps us to identify the full quality of our personal being so we can accomplish the passion, purpose and potential that we came to this plane with as our mission in this life. You may have tried to accomplish this particular mission before and gotten blocked by others, or blocked yourself from the fears of being ridiculed for being different or for not fitting in with the norm. You may have tried to meet others' expectations. It could have been as simple as someone telling you, or placing their agenda on you:

- "You can't do that; you have to do this."
- "Don't feel that way."
- "Get over it."

- "Grow up."

It is my intention in this book to help you identify the quality of your numbers. You will be able to identify your personal qualities, which will liberate you and give you permission to be free to be all that you can be. You will be free to discover that who you are—and who you have been told that you are—may be very different.

Darlene Chadbourne

Freedom

Numerology helps you discover freedom. We all began to formulate our identity while living within our mother's energy. Therefore we may need to question some of our basic beliefs.

- Are we afraid to be free?
- Are we always seeking to be in relationship with someone else's energy, like the mother?
- Do we feel vulnerable and alone in the world? Are we afraid of leaving the safe, warm, and dark environment?
- Are we afraid of being alone, cut off from our original life support?

When the soul comes into a physical body it has to learn how to operate that body. The soul is confined to one body that needs another to supply its basic needs. This is where we start our mission of helping the family that we have been born into.

- Are there members in this family who are jealous of our arrival and resentful of our being here?
- Are they jealous of the attention we need in order to survive?
- Are there circumstances that we are born into that require us to be abandoned, given away, or neglected?

- Does this make the soul feel like it was a mistake to choose this family at this time?

Or are you loved and caressed and honored as the most beautiful and wonderful product of love ever produced? Were you loved all through your in utero experience knowing that this family was well prepared to accept you, love you, adore you, and support you; did you arrive knowing you were so wanted and cherished?

- Was your entrance into this earth plane on your terms or was it according to someone else's time schedule?
- Did they wait for you to decide to be ready to leave the womb or were you taken out before your perfect time was reached?
- Was your transition smooth and easy or full of anxiety and emergency conditions?

There are many ways of healing and reworking these events around your birth to attain the freedom you deserve.

Naming a newborn is a long process of many considerations and lots of input from many sources. Ultimately it is usually the mother that knows the right name for the baby that has been within her for nine months. The outside pressures of using a family name, or tagging a junior to the end, lock this newborn into a pattern that has already been established by someone else. It is defining and limiting to say the least. It

Darlene Chadbourne

is implying that you have to be like your father or like Aunt Susie, or like someone six generations into the past. It takes away the freedom and spontaneity of being your own person. It may cause you to rebel for unknown reasons. It may take you until a midlife crisis to give yourself permission to step into your own uniqueness and away from everyone else's expectations of you, or maybe you rebelled early and struck out on your own to seek your freedom and identity.

The more you know, or can find out, about the circumstances of your conception, your in-utero experiences, your birth, and your name the more light you will shine on the ways that you act and the ways that you respond to situations in your own personal life.

Numerology can always bring you information about who you came into this earth plane to be and permission to liberate your gifts as joyful fuel for the rest of your journey in this lifetime. Numerology can help you label the jewels within your being and within this lifetime of experiences. The blueprint is the blending of all of your precious jewels in this lifetime. Take all of your jewels out of each of the rooms in your blueprint and be the alchemist blending and mixing. Then trust being open to the new pleasure and joy of being all that you are and all that you can be. Rising up to the occasion, be the Star that you are. Your blueprint is your structure, that container that holds your power, your "I AM"! Create a joyful time-out in your meditation room to listen and receive what is yours to be.

Pull together your own personal presence, your own power from your blueprint. Trust, though, that once you step into it, you will need to share your story because it is a piece of the whole; if everyone shared their story the world would live as one. There is room for all. Working with this personal presence through meditation or journaling is helpful (see Tools on page 185).

Many trends in history have to do with a quest for more and more possessions, as the popular saying goes, "the one with the most toys wins." This type of statement suggests that *quantity* is the deciding factor in a success equation. We see this philosophy of "more is better" and greed for power in current events taking place around the world. How will history be written about the current events that we are living? Will whoever has the most money, toys, and power in the world be the guideline used to determine success forever?

Through this book I will show you how to work your numbers by activating the Blueprint number you want to focus on, to attain the freedom that you deserve and are meant to have during your lifetime.

Chapter 2

Native Path Method: Worksheet, Chart, and Blueprint

A **chart** signifies that you know your personal number combination, but does not call for any action.

A **worksheet** states your personal number combination that you have to work with, but it doesn't give you the view of the goals set before you to work through in order to see the finished product.

A **blueprint** is a specific action plan of what your personal life is aiming to look like for you and your ability to achieve it. The **blueprint** gives you the description of what room to go to, to effect a change.

As you read the instructions refer to:

The Letter to Number Conversion Chart, p. 54

The Blueprint, p. 65

Worksheets, p. 66-67.

The Blueprint

Creating a numerology blueprint is a building project much like building a house. Join me in stretching your imagination and let's use this as a metaphor for building your personal blueprint.

The whole house appears from the outside as one single item, but what is found inside that house are many rooms, each with its own purpose and definition. Each room has a unique placement, shape, décor, energy and specific purpose. The layout and décor give it a personality that is different from any other structure, even those that may look the same from the outside. The eight blueprint positions are similar to rooms within your unique structure.

As you build your personal numerology blueprint you begin to see the placement, shape, décor, energy and purpose coming into form and the unique characteristics of who you have the potential to be and to build on.

Knowing your numbers is one thing; to familiarize yourself with each of your numbers as a lens, and learn how to use it to look at your world, is another. In this context there are the numbers 1-9, and then there is "0", which is an amplifier.

The next step is knowing your blueprint positions or the rooms in your personalized house, and where each of the numbers resides in your life. These blueprint positions can help to determine the time frame—past, present, or future—signifying

Darlene Chadbourne

when the numbers need to be activated or when they need to be kept in reserve for future use.

The standard rule in numerology is reducing totals by simple addition to a single digit (23/5 means 2 + 3 = 5) however, I prefer leaving the equation whole as it helps with interpretations. A twin digit Master Number is the exception to the rule and looks like (22/4 means 2 + 2 = 4). A Master Number is left to read 22/4, rather than the single digit. While all positions in the Blueprint are important they do have an order of importance. The following is the typical order of importance:

- Native Path
- Birthday number
- Path of Destiny
- Soul
- Personality
- Maturity
- Inner Guidance
- Fulfillment
- Career/Success

That being said, the Blueprint positions on the worksheet are placed in a different order for the ease of calculating the simple arithmetic. For this purpose we will look at them in this order:

Freedom Through Numbers

- Soul
- Personality
- Path of Destiny
- Inner Guidance
- Native Path
- Maturity
- Career/Success
- Fulfillment

∞

(Blank Blueprint form is on page 65)

Working the Calculations

The language of Numerology, Astrology, and Kabala has appeared throughout history. In fact, numbers are important enough in the Bible that there is an entire book devoted to Biblical numerology.

Numbers are Mathematical Symbols* carrying meaning in the form of characteristics and traits that we recognize as archetypes relative to behaviors, habits, and personalities. When we transpose the letters of our alphabet into the numbers of 1 to 26, we identify their numerical vibration or energy signature. We then revert to the simplicity of our early mathematical education of addition to calculate the totals for each of the positions in the Blueprint.

*(Ideas gained from Steven Scott Pither's *The Complete Book of Numbers*)

Letter-to-Number Conversion Chart

This is the Chart you will use to change letters to numbers in your name.

1	2	3	4	5	6	7	8	9
A	B	C	D	E	F	G	H	I
J	K	L	M	N	O	P	Q	R
S	T	U	V	W	X	Y	Z	
1	2	3	4	5	6	7	8	9

Next I will explain what each Blueprint position means. It will give you a much better understanding of the means within the positions.

Darlene Chadbourne

Soul Number is your room of memories, gifts and talents that you have brought into this lifetime experience. It is your job to use them to enhance and expand this lifetime experience. It is a hidden part of your personality.

The Soul number is an important core influence in numerology. You don't expose this number to those around you. It is your inner cravings, likes and dislikes, which are usually kept private. This is the number that represents what you value most. This is the nature that drives you in your everyday life. Satisfying this number will give you a sense of inner peace and contentment.

Soul number is your gifts and talents that come naturally to you. Some refer to these as God-given gifts. The theory is that you already learned these gifts in the soul's previous incarnations.

Time:

Past tense—What did you bring in with you from previous experiences?

All Calculations for your Soul number are derived from the Pythagorean Letter to Number Conversion Chart using the Vowels in your Full Name at Birth.

Calculation: Soul number =

Total of the numerical vibration of the Vowels in your Full Name at Birth.

Personality Number is the room that you invite others into so you can show them the parts of you that you want them to see. This is the part of you that shines out to the rest of the world like a beacon, magnetizing people to you like the marquee on the old style theaters. It is the "Your Name in Lights" section of your life. This is the room where you totally interact with others in the outside world.

Strangely, this number is also associated with your personality in terms of how people see you on first meetings. This number may be so strong in your subconscious that you even project the trait as a personality mask. It is better to shine your light out to the world as a beacon of who you are.

Time:

Present Tense — Living in the Now.

All Calculations for your Personality number are derived from the Pythagorean Letter to Number Conversion Chart using the Consonants in your Full Name at Birth.

Calculation: Personality =

Total of the numerical vibration of the Consonants in your Full Name at Birth.

Darlene Chadbourne

Path of Destiny Number is the room with the drafting table and plans for what you want to build during this lifetime. Your future goals reside here. It is where you want to end up in the later years of your life, a trajectory number that moves you forward to your goals for this lifetime. This number is active until we leave this world. Knowing what the vibration of this number is and reaching for it helps to enhance your purpose for being here in this lifetime—what are you hoping to accomplish in the future? This number gives you a broad sense of where you need to put your focus.

Time:

Future Tense — Looking forward to your hopes and dreams.

Path of Destiny number is Future Tense, building toward a goal and reaching for your personal accomplishment.

All Calculations for your Path of Destiny number are derived from the Pythagorean Letter to Number Conversion Chart using the *vowels* and *consonants* in your Full Name at Birth.

Calculations: Total of your Soul and Personality numbers = Path of Destiny.

Inner Guidance Number (Thank you to Shirley Blackwell Lawrence, who wrote *The Secret Science of Numerology, The Hidden Meaning of Numbers and Letters*. She developed this numerology blueprint position, which is so needed in this 21st century and our current changing times—see p. 263 of her book.) The Inner Guidance number is like your meditation room where you use this trait to access your higher self and messages from *Source* or *All That Is*. It is your intuition room. If you take the time to meditate in it, this is the number that takes you to a higher octave. Meditating here develops your intuition, tapping into outer dimensions of timelessness, to outer world guides, angels, and helpers, out in "No Time—All That Is." This is how you connect and hear your intuitive connection.

Time:

Past, Present, & Future Tense

Calculations: Path of Destiny x 2.

The previous four rooms:
- Soul
- Personality
- Path of Destiny
- Inner Guidance

These are all constructed from the numbers vibrating in your full name at birth.

Darlene Chadbourne

Native Path Number is the room where you step into the universal time machine which has been running continuously for eons. The Native Path is the date of your nativity, where your soul decides to enter this time machine of Earth, and start life as an individual. This is the moment when you separated from your physical mother and grounded to the Earth mother. This number introduces you to the lessons that you will encounter in your lifetime.

It is the room that starts your personal clock that meshes with the universal clock in the perfect place for you to begin your journey. Think of this room as having multiple clocks and calendars in it. This is the starting place for all of your future moves, creating the timing of events and all of your milestones. You chose this time and place to enter the world in order to expand your soul's experiences and to evolve to the next level. Timing and Logistics belong here.

Time:

Present Tense — Tapping into the universal time clock of now.

It is derived only from your arrival date, your full date of birth.

Calculations:

Month (1 or 2 digits) + birthday (1 or 2 digits) + year (4 digits) = Native Path

Maturity Number is the room where you grow into your purpose and focus on the plan you created for yourself before you came into this lifetime. You spend time in this room between ages 35-65 (midlife time).

Maturity Path is a futuristic number, the carrot at the end of the stick that you are always reaching to attain, to improve your life.

It is the midlife number, relating to those years between 35-65, when you start your search for the real you, otherwise called "midlife." A time of redrafting and rebuilding your beliefs and the foundation of the real you. The other trajectory number to help you build your goals.

The Magic of 50 is right smack dab in the middle between 35 and 65. The combination of the 5 as a free spirit and the 0 as—spirit has your back—can give you the jet propulsion that you need to make the changes to create the new structure for the rest of your life. Please notice that each of these double digit numbers (35-50-65) have a 5 as an energy within them. (5 is the number of change, freedom, and the power of the written word.)

Time: Present Tense — Doing it your way.

Calculations:

Path of Destiny + Native Path = Maturity Path

Darlene Chadbourne

Career/Success Number is the room that exhibits the maps and routes for you to take to accomplish your mission. It is the Mission Control room that draws all the information together to make it a whole work in progress.

Career Success means reaching for success in your passion and purpose of the work you are here to do. Everything done in the present builds toward the future that is yours to have and thrive in, defining what is yours to do and how to do it in order to accomplish this phase of your soul's journey. This is the bigger picture of who you are and what you are doing here, your Self-Importance piece.

Time:

Present Tense and Future Tense. What you aspire to in this lifetime.

Calculation:

Soul + Personality + Path of Destiny + Native Path = Career/Success

Fulfillment Number is the room that you go to, in order to witness the progress and feel the satisfaction of a job well done. It is the trophy room of all of your achievements. It is the room that holds your multiple awards for a job well done. It is where you feel fulfilled and as though you have accomplished something. Satisfaction is what this number seeks to bring into your life. This number gives you a clue as to where to seek that fulfillment; what brings you joy and happiness, what makes your soul sing, what makes you feel on top of the world. Like a kite with the freedom to soar, with a slight string tethering it to the Earth.

Time:

Present Tense. What makes you feel satisfied and fulfilled?

Calculation:

Birth Month + Birth Day = Fulfillment

Now that you have been introduced to the rooms or positions in your Blueprint, how will you master:

- your Soul's gifts
- your Personality's radiance
- your Path of Destiny's goals
- your Inner Guidance's presence
- your Native Path's time machine
- your Maturity's distinction
- your Career/Success's achievements
- your Fulfillment's satisfaction?

When you master your numbers, you can then leave your personal signature on your lifetime, saying, "I came, I saw, I loved, I conquered all the parts of myself by *Naming, Claiming, and Becoming* the full master of my life." This is the freedom you are looking for.

Now that you have a visual of your blueprint we can look at the mechanics and figures of how to define them.

NOTES:

Numerology Blueprint

```
1 2 3 4 5 6 7 8 9
A B C D E F G H I
J K L M N O P Q R
S T U V W X Y Z
1 2 3 4 5 6 7 8 9
```

                                                              SOUL   #

Full Name at Birth:

                                                  PERSONALITY   #

                                                  PATH OF DESTINY   #

                                                  INNER GUIDANCE   #

Date of Birth: **NATIVE PATH**   #

                                                  MATURITY PATH   #

                                                  CAREER/SUCCESS   #

                                                  FULFILLMENT   #

Freedom Through Numbers

Worksheet Calculations for your Blueprint

1. Full Name at Birth

2. Vowels = Soul

3. Consonants = Personality

4. Total of Vowels + Consonants = Path of Destiny

5. Path of Destiny x 2 = Inner Guidance

6. Date of Birth
 Month (1 or 2 digits) + Day (1 or 2 digits) + Year (4 digits) = Native Path

7. Total of Path of Destiny + Native Path = Maturity

8. Soul + Personality + Path of Destiny + Native Path = Career/Success

9. Birth Month + Birthday = Fulfillment

Numerology Blueprint

```
1 2 3 4 5 6 7 8 9
A B C D E F G H I
J K L M N O P Q R
S T U V W X Y Z
1 2 3 4 5 6 7 8 9
```

                        SOUL   #

Full Name at Birth:

                        PERSONALITY   #

                        PATH OF DESTINY   #

                        INNER GUIDANCE   #

Date of Birth:

                        NATIVE PATH   #

                        MATURITY PATH   #

                        CAREER/SUCCESS   #

                        FULFILLMENT   #

Darlene Chadbourne

Figuring Your Numbers

You start with your full name at birth and the date of birth as written on your birth certificate.

There are different ways to calculate the numbers. I have labeled them with the results as A, B, C, D.

A reminder:

The standard rule in numerology is reducing totals by simple addition to a single digit (23/5 means 2 + 3 = 5). I prefer leaving the whole equation, as it helps with interpretations. A twin digit Master Number is the exception to the rule, and looks like this: 22/4 (means 2 + 2 = 4). In this case it is left to read 22/4, the whole equation rather than the single digit.

Reducing is a rule in numerology that has, in the past, been strictly adhered to. I have discovered in my practice that if you always reduce everything, you miss many of the available master numbers and zeros. The master numbers and zeros explain many of the complexities and helpful uplifting energies available to a person. After all, we are complex beings. Life is not as simple as a single number.

Early on in my practice of numerology I noticed that although multiple people could be a 5 they didn't all have the same traits that brought them to be a 5. Simply put, they had all arrived at the 5 but they had each taken a different route to get there. For example, one might have a 23/5 which would use the 2 energy of teamwork and cooperation combined with the 3 energy of creative expression. Another person might have a 41/5 which would use the 4 grounded material world energy of step-by-step building and the 1 of leadership and confidence in guiding or teaching others, to attain the freedom of the 5 energy. It helps to think of the numbers preceding the diagonal as adjectives that enrich the understanding through their descriptive value of how the single digit is reached.

These adjective numbers work in the background and become especially important when you first begin interpreting the numbers for you or someone else. A good example of this is the difference between a 22/4 a master number (22) and a 40/4 with the zero. While these are both 4 energies they take very different routes to get to the 4. The 22 is about building relationships and taking your intuitive abilities and learning to apply them for physical manifestation. The 40 is about allowing the zero that accompanies the 4 to uplift it to a higher spiritual level. Looking to the elusive spiritual realm to enhance the material world.

The following graph will help you see the four different ways to calculate the numbers. I have labeled them A, B, C, D.

The single digit behind the diagonal should result in the same number for all four ways. If it is not, then there is a calculating error somewhere in the addition.

Darlene Chadbourne

For demonstration purposes we will use the following birthday as an example: November 25, 1946

   11 -- 25 -- 1946

A. Adds each of the single digits in the date of birth horizontally = 29/11/2.

      A. 1+1 + 2+5 + 1+9+4+6 = 29/11/2*

B. Adds the month 11, the date 25, and the year 1946 without reducing in a column. The total becomes 1982, which then is reduced to a 20/2.

C. Does not reduce the 11 (master number), reduces the 25 to a 7, and the year to a 20, totaling them in a vertical column = 38/11/2.

D. Reduces the month 11 to a 2, the date 25 to a 7, and the year to a 2 = 11/2.

		B.	C.	D.
Month	November	11	11	2
Day	25	+25	07	7
Year	1946	1+9+4+6=	20	2
		1982		
		1+9+8+2=20/2*	38/11/2*	11/2*

Freedom Through Numbers
~ 71 ~

* Examples A, B, C, D, show four different ways of calculating.

If this was calculated by only one of the three ways, you may not have found the 20/2. Sometimes you find a number with one of the digits being a zero, which lends a high spiritual vibration to the number it is with. The *magic* comes from the zero (0) working together with the 2 to enhance the free spirit and energy of networking, team work, and relationships. I like to say, "Spirit has your back" when the zero shows up.

It is also worth exploring that in this example three of the four ways of calculating have produced a twin digits, the Master Number 11. The majority of the time expanding out the math will reveal different double digit numbers proceeding the same single digit; and every time that happens you will say to yourself, "Why did I take the time to figure it four ways?!" That is the reason that I have used this particular birthday in my example, so you will know what the possibilities are and what you might be missing if you do it only one way.

Darlene Chadbourne

Discovering Your Numbers

Using your Date of Birth, the total becomes your Native Path number. Now repeat steps A, B, C, and D to calculate your Native Path number as per the example on page 71.

Next, use your full name at birth with the alphabet chart on the next page.

Calculate your personal Blueprint numbers in order to help you realize your full potential.

The numbers hold the information as to how you respond to the world around you by identifying your personal traits, gifts, and talents.

Numerology allows you to revisit and celebrate the importance of your arrival as an individual on planet Earth.

When you first disconnect from your mother and become an individual it is the beginning point that you set up for your personal energy vibration and your personal time cycles for life.

Letter-to-Number Conversion Chart

1	2	3	4	5	6	7	8	9
A	B	C	D	E	F	G	H	I
J	K	L	M	N	O	P	Q	R
S	T	U	V	W	X	Y	Z	
1	2	3	4	5	6	7	8	9

Darlene Chadbourne

"According to Pythagoras, true 'happiness consists in knowledge of perfection of the numbers of the soul.'"–*The Pythagorean Sourcebook and Library*, Guthrie & Fideler, 1987, Phanes Press, Grand Rapids, Michigan 49516, USA. p. 33.

"The Pythagoreans divided the study of Number into four branches which may be analyzed in the following fashion:

Arithmetic = Number in itself.

Geometry = Number in space.

Music or Harmonics = Number in time.

Astronomy = Number in space and time."

p.34, Ibid

This is referred to as the quadrivium.

"The symbolism finds its basis in the Pythagorean observation that the primary numbers represent far more than quantitative signs; each one of the primary numbers is a qualitative, archetypal essence, possessing a distinct, living personality. This personality can be directly intuited by studying the archetypal manifestations of these principles in the realms arithmetic (number in itself), geometry (number in space) and harmonics (number in time)."

Ibid, p. 321

Now let's calculate the numbers of the name. For this example we will use the following name:

David Allen Major

And let's do each name separately:

	First Name		
Vowels	1 + 9 = 10/1	10/1	1
	D **a** v **i** d		
	D a **v** i **d**		
Consonants	4 + 4 + 4 = 12/3	+12/3	+3
Total		22/4	4

Assign a number to each of the vowels in the name, on the line above the name, using the Letter-to-Number Conversion Chart. Notice, the a and i are bolded.

Assign the corresponding number to each of the consonants in the name, referencing the chart, and write those numbers on the bottom line under the name. Notice, The d, v and d are bolded.

Darlene Chadbourne

Now calculate the middle name. (If there is more than one middle name, put them together and treat them as one.)

	Middle * Name		
Vowels	1 + 5 =	6	6
	A l l e n		
	A l l e n		
Consonants	3+3 +5=	+ 11/2	+2
Total		17/8	8

Assign the corresponding number to each of the vowels in the name, referencing the chart, and write those numbers on the line above the name. Notice, the a and e are bolded.

Assign the corresponding number to each of the consonants in the name, referencing the chart, and write those numbers on the bottom line under the name. Notice, the l, l and n are bolded.

Freedom Through Numbers

Check every combination to find master numbers or zeros.

Then, calculate the last name:

	Surname		
Vowels	1 + 6 = 7	7	7
	M **a** j **o** r		
	M a **j** o **r**		
Consonants	4 + 1 + 9 = 14/5	+14	+5
Total		21/3	12/3

Assign the corresponding number to each of the vowels in the name, referencing the chart, and write those numbers on the line above the name. Notice, the a and o are bolded.

Assign the corresponding number to each of the consonants in the name, referencing the chart, and write those numbers on the bottom line under the name. Notice, the M, j and r are bolded

Check every combination to find master numbers or zeros.

The total of the **vowels** for all three names: 10/1 + 6 + 7 = 23/5.

This **23/5** is the **Soul** number in the Blueprint.

Now do the same with the **consonants**.

The total of the consonants for all three names:

12/3 + 11/2 + 14/5 = 37/10/1.

This **37/10/1** is the **Personality** number in the Blueprint.

Both zeros and a master number appear in the full name.

Now add the **23/5** of the **Soul** number and the **37/10/1** of the **Personality** number together and **60/6** is the total of the 23 + 37 all of the letters in the full name which is the **Path of Destiny** number in the Blueprint. Let's try one more combination of numbers for the total 23 + 10 = 33/6, a master number. Both of these numbers need to be considered as part of the **Path of Destiny**.

If this was calculated only one of the three ways, you may not have found the 33/6, a Master Number. Or 60/6 with one of the digits being a zero, which lends a high spiritual vibration to the number it is with. The Magic comes from the 0 working together with the 6 to show that "Spirit has your back."

Multiplying the Path of Destiny number by 2 gives you your Inner Guidance number.

You have now learned to calculate four of the eight numbers of the Blueprint: Soul number, Personality number, Path of Destiny number, and Inner Guidance number. Now calculate your own full name at birth.

You are halfway to identifying your full, true identity or the Freedom to be all that you can be!

See your calculations on the next page to find your way to the last three numbers in the Blueprint: Maturity Path, Career/Success, and Fulfillment.

Calculations for Your Blueprint

- Full Name at Birth
- Vowels = Soul
- Consonants = Personality
- Total of Vowels + Consonants = Path of Destiny
- Path of Destiny x 2 = Inner Guidance
- Date of Birth, Month + Day + Year = Native Path
- Total of Path of Destiny + Native Path = Maturity
- Total of four digits of the Current Year = Universal Energy
- Birth Month + Birth Day + Current Year = Personal Year Energy
- Soul + Personality + Path of Destiny + Native Path = Career/Success
- Birth Month + Birth Day = Fulfillment

Freedom Through Numbers

After the Blueprint

- Determine what your blueprint numbers are.
- Research the meaning or trait of each of the numbers.
- Pay attention to the position that each number occupies.

If the results seem familiar to you and you can identify it as a trait that you possess, great. This means you are already owning this trait as a part of your overall being.

If you do not see this as a part of who you are and feel that you would like to be more like this trait, the next step would be to ask yourself what is blocking you from owning this part of yourself.

The only time this would not apply is if you were born an hour one side or the other of midnight. If this is the case, calculate a new blueprint with the day before or after midnight and refer to my chapter on timing and the soul's either/or timeline. You would then choose which of the two blueprints feels more like who you can identify with or seems more like you.

I have only had this happen a few times in my career. A person says, "That is nothing like me." I then ask them if they know their time of birth. Each time they came back with a time that was within an hour of midnight. Once I calculated the blueprint

Darlene Chadbourne

for the day on the other side of midnight they could identify with it very well. Since that time I have requested the time of birth as a part of a client's original information.

Darlene Chadbourne

Chapter 3

The Meanings of the Numbers

Zero: The Cosmic Egg (full of all potential)—all numbers come from it.

0 represents spirit in all applications. After all, everything that has ever existed has come from nothing. I firmly believe this. Through my experiences of the last twenty years of calculating numerology blueprints, I have also recognized the fact that Zero is everything and nothing at the same time. I was brought up with the concept that you cannot see God, but he is everywhere. Nothingness has a right to claim a space in the number sequence as it uplifts the number it is with to a higher level of spirituality. I feel that everything is born of the *Cosmic Egg* of nothingness, or unlimited possibilities. All numbers come from that *Cosmic Egg* of everything and nothing or no thing.

I find it unusual that during my graduation study for my thesis, I created a watercolor, and even then I wanted to name it the Cosmic Egg (see the watercolor on the back cover).

ZERO represents the ending and the beginning.

When the zero is added to represent the 10 space, it signifies the end of the single digit numbers and the beginning of the tens. As in the 20, it is the ending of the teens, the second round of tens in the 20s and the beginning of the thirties and so on and so forth.

- Is this where spirit or source resides in the space between the ending and the beginning?
- Is this why we need to go to the 0 space or nothingness space of meditation to experience spirit?
- Is the zero representative of the space between the worlds of existence?
- When we are in that zero space are we in touch with spirit?
- Does the zero space hold the answers to all questions and possibilities?
- Is this why we are in the process of change ever since we have crossed into the new millennium with 2000s three zeros or the two zeros in 2002?

As I write this, we've just entered 2020. These important milestone years are the time to take a leap of faith and be like the innocent Fool card in the tarot deck. By becoming everything and nothing all at the same time, you enter the world of possibilities.

This is why we feel the zeros as we turn each decade in our age. That is when we leave one milestone of accomplishment in the past decade and we look forward to all of the new possibilities and opportunities in the new decade.

Darlene Chadbourne
~ 86 ~

Single Digits 1-9

1 is about your *Self-importance*, not ego or arrogance. My description of *Self-importance* is to claim that you were born into this world for a purpose and you intend to fulfill that purpose. Many people who carry this number 1 vibration are on opposite ends of the spectrum with it. They are either very egotistical and arrogant. Or they refuse to step into their power for fear of abusing the power, which leads to other people walking all over them by taking advantage of their vulnerability. If you do not own your power in a healthy way, it can come back to bite you in an uncomfortable situation. Number 1's need this power to accomplish their mission in this lifetime but are so afraid of hurting someone that they disown it.

The secret here is to apply your power in a healthy manner with your gifts and talents that you were born with. Get familiar with both sides of the either/or concept, then find the middle ground. Once you have done this, review your past and see where you have been living and using your number 1 vibration. Now get yourself into a positive mind frame so you can create positive affirmations about the direction and place you see yourself in going forward. Go to Appendix 4 for the list of words that vibrate to the number one energy. Look to see if you have a number 1 in your blueprint as the last number in the equation. What blueprint position is it in?

The equations are derived from the total that comes from adding the letter vibrations together in each of the positions. Use the whole equation because it helps in the interpretation of the single digit it is reduced to. Then look at the whole equation that precedes the one.

Match that number equation to the same number equation column in the appendix. Choose one of the words from that list of words in that column. There is a separate column for each total that reduces to a 10, then reduces to a 1. The reductions are always separated by a forward slash /.

Number 1—leader, initiator, new ideas, head of the operation, can stand up in front of the crowd, can stay centered and focused, allow the world to turn around you, release control, eliminate chaos, find peace and harmony in stillness, draw people and things to you.

Opposites:

Egotistic, selfish, greedy, tyrant, power over others, mean, oppressor, wants the spotlight on self, has a "me, myself, and I" attitude and lack of consideration for others.

2 refers to duality—the 1 became two in order to observe and know the self. The number 2 is very good at working with others in any capacity. Their concern is about the other and what the other person thinks about them. Or what they can do for that other person. They make a great mediator, counselor, negotiator, or team player. A business needs a lot of number 2 personalities working together to have things run smoothly. But they are wise to have only one number 1 personality as the department leader, otherwise there will be clashes as to who is in control.

Number 2 people support others through cooperation and companionship. They are great in relationships because of their patience in getting the job done. They can epitomize duality and play both sides of the fence, and know how to work with all kinds of personalities.

Number 2—the power behind the throne, works well with others, peacemaker, conflict resolution, negotiator, politician, partner, base decisions on intuition, sensitive, arbitrator, balancer, team player, facilitator, committee person, mediator, counselor, team player, joiner, always searching for the other, peace at all cost, supporter of others, negotiator, interrogator, closing the deal with all sides happy.

Opposites:

One-sided, either/or thought process, creates or stirs up conflict, argues over everything, dualistic, always negative, conflicted.

3 people are the happy-go-lucky cheerleaders of the world and unusually upbeat. Years ago there was a doll that was produced, like many dolls before it, to look like and to do things that real people did. This particular holiday season was the year of the "Chatty Cathy," a talking doll that would go on and on. This might have been the beginning of the talking robot technology, without the intelligence part.

Number 3 people have an easy time talking to people, in front of people, on stage, in performance mode. Music is a strength for a number 3. If they are not encouraged to get involved with singing or a musical instrument early in life, they could pursue it later in life. They have a very good ear for music and they should at the very least enjoy listening to music a good part of the day.

They can have a tendency to get on their soapbox and talk non-stop until someone else asks them to stop. Or until no one is around to listen any more. They make very vocal lawyers, politicians, orators, teachers, actors, singers, and performers of any type. Out of all the 1-9 numbers 3's make the best clowns, in fact they were probably the class clown if they were allowed to be themselves. It also helped if they had a number 1 energy in another blueprint position.

Number 3 people cannot stand to see others depressed or sad. They instantly go into cheerleader mode. They are the people that throw a party on the spur of the moment without a care in the world. They have full confidence that everything will work out perfectly, even if it looks like a chaotic mess.

Darlene Chadbourne

Number 3's are very creative, and most creativity starts with chaos. The opposite side of the coin for number 3 energy people is that they can get stuck in the chaos and never be able to see their way clear to find the method for reorganizing the chaos into order. Then they feel stuck not being able to find their way out of the situation.

Number 3's need to stay very active so they do not stagnate in inertia, and yet the answers for them come as they sit quietly and listen, which is the hardest thing for them to do.

The following are their hardest challenges:
- To listen for incoming messages.
- To sit in an audience and pay attention to others talk.
- To not respond to another comment.
- To not turn conversations into debates.
- To be silent.
- To listen to others.

Number 3—creator, communicator, performer, speaker, class clown, cheerleader, crafter, full of joy, happy go lucky, playful, easy going, imaginative, self-expressive, creative clutter, talkative, artistic, loves to be in groups.

Opposites:

Scattered, flaky, flamboyant, demonstrative, lack of creativity, blah, heavy hearted, moody.

A number **4** person is one you want on your side. They know how to work long and hard with a stick-to-it attitude until it is done. They make a great manager for teamwork positions. They can be stoic and a workaholic and downright boring, but good at taking care of the mundane details. They are natural builders as long as they start with a good solid foundation, proceeding in a step-by-step fashion, being careful not to miss a step. The number 4 has a knack for organizing unless some of their other numbers sway them away from that trait. Practical, steady, and secure in relationships, but need to be reminded to lighten up and have some fun.

Number 4—To build and manifest in the material world, solid, secure, foundation, square, four corners, cornerstone, cross-roads, organized, stabilized, work, container, limiting, caretaker for others.

Opposites:

Workaholic, rigid, stubborn, bearing a cross, burdened, heavy, stuck, martyr.

A number **5** person wants to be a free spirit. Their motto is, "Don't tie me down." They have a difficult time staying grounded. They want to be in the airy-fairy world, observing like a fly on the wall. They do not like to make commitments.

Number 5's make good salespersons as they have a skill with words and can talk to anyone about anything. Foreign languages come easy to them. Both the spoken and written word is their forte. They make great news reporters, journalists, and authors. They seek jobs that are attached to lots of travel. They would also be a good travel agent.

Number 5's are the original roadrunners; they cannot sit still. Movement is essential for their wellbeing. They are agents for change, especially when it comes up as a temporary vibration. If you think about when the numbers 1 through 9 are lined up in a row. (1 2 3 4 5 6 7 8 9), 5 is right in the middle with 4 numbers to the left and 4 numbers to the right. The 5 has the best overview for looking forward and backward. It is not attached to the past or the future, but very content in the present and going with the flow.

Number 5 is connected to sexuality and addictions, mainly because they are not grounded in their own energy so they look to something outside of themselves to ground them. They are very sensitive and operate well through the five senses.

Number 5—Free spirit, sensitive, sexual, sensual, guide for wisdom, teacher, salesperson, traveler, language, written word, media, advertising, adaptable, a channel, liberation, limitless possibilities, free of attachment to outcome, school, (human being has five extremities, Head, 2 hands, 2 feet like DaVinci's Vitruvian Man), awareness through 5 senses. Airy-fairy, unfocused, ungrounded, "Don't tie me down," freedom, gift of gab, mentally sharp, college material, verbally fluent, foreign languages, words, speaker, speech, communication, writing, press, loves change, easily bored.

Opposites:

Oppression, false images, setbacks, disappointment, addictions, lack of grounding. Addictive personality, needs to be grounded to avoid addictions.

A number **6** person is the ultimate caretaker, and more times than not at their own expense. Their priority is to serve others in professions such as nurse, doctor, Massage therapist, Reiki practitioner, mothering and caretaking others is their specialty. They can be masters at self-sacrifice for others or mother hens that hover over their children, not allowing them the freedom they need. It is finding a balance point between the extremes of micro managing versus not caring.

This person can also be the home-body that doesn't want to leave the house. They are very content with household chores and nurturing others. So it is no surprise that marriage and divorce come under this energy. Number 6 is a family-first kind of energy. They are very responsible—you can trust them to take care of a person, a situation or a job.

The other very strong energy for them is music, whether it be playing and performing or listening for relaxation. They need the harmony and balance that music provides.

Number 6 people love to love and be loved. They also love beauty whether it be in the garden with landscaping or in the home with color or feng shui for balancing the energy. They have an eye for harmony and balance through design. They make great interior decorators or clothing designers.

Number 6—Harmony, balance, horizon, beauty, family, children, health, healing, landscape, interior design, visual, music, art, equality, love, balancing duality; male/female balance, sunrise/sunset, being fair, medical, nursing, healing arts, nurturing others. Marriage, divorce, mother, father, loving, nurturing, health, self-sacrificing, artistic, musical instruments, decorating, gardening, feng shui, harmony and balance. Hands-on healers, massage, nurses, doctors, alternative therapies.

Opposites:

Judgmental, possessive, nosy, one-sided, unbalanced, narcissistic.

A number **7** person needs alone time. They need the freedom to say, "Give me 15-30 minutes by myself and then I will be able to be here for you." Those alone minutes are precious to them. They are the ancient-philosopher type who observes and is able to retain lots of knowledge. They like being the lifetime student, always looking for another class or degree to attain more knowledge.

They might be called the mystic or Merlin the magician type. Studious and quiet, or the geek that loves to get involved in a project and to be able to have all the answers for people's problems. They especially love ancient knowledge and life's mysteries and how nature works, like the astrologer or astronomer, teacher and student. We might call them odd or eccentric, especially if they are withdrawn, or shy, knowing that they are different and not knowing why.

They might be involved in the spiritual or metaphysical world of mysterious and unseen phenomena. Science and technology is their comfort place, to immerse themselves in, so they don't have to deal with people. They could be the geniuses of the world, if left alone to pursue their inner knowledge and intuitive knowing— they could be the next greatest inventor.

They love books and would be a good librarian and research technician. They can be skeptical of people and very private.

Darlene Chadbourne

Number 7—Quiet, presence, studious, contemplative, deep thought, philosophy, curiosity, teacher/student, education, retreat, meditation, monk, nun, priest, priestess, unlearned, faith, belief, mystical, peace, tranquility, recluse, lifetime student, teacher, school, deep thinker, knowledge, hunger for more knowledge, ancient knowledge, alternative health, yoga, quiet, withdrawn, silence, cloister, vows, content at home, introvert.

Opposites: Avoidance, busy bee.

A number **8** person is the great multitasker with the ability to do things faster, more efficiently, with better results than anyone giving them orders, trying to micro-manage their performance. The number 8 person also excels in the financial world. It has been said that they can make a million and lose a million and make another million.

They make great organizers and leaders, better the boss than the employee. Give them the trust and freedom to do it their way and they excel. They really know how to manifest and create something out of nothing. They are good with numbers as accountants and financiers. I would call this number 8 the master minds of the world. They thrive on the details, so if they have all the details they can make most anything work. They are great analyzers and problem solvers. They can also see the larger picture of where a project is going. They know future trends before they happen. They seek material success as a part of their fulfillment. They need the whole picture with all the details to produce the best results.

Number 8—Flow, trust, above and below, working together, business, finances, self-employed, multitasking, in unison, wealth, money, management, consciousness, abundance, balance, achieved and accomplished, balancing of above and below, need both not one or the other, heaven and earth, joined at the heart, flow, flow chart, emotions. Authority figure, entrepreneur, owner, manager, big boss, business, multitasker, wheeler and dealer, can handle many things at once, will get it done fast, more efficiently, with better results if left alone with no micro-managing.

Opposites:

Stagnant, loss, poverty, conflict with others, judgmental, criticism.

A number **9** person is a humanitarian, who loves nature and animals and the down trodden, and will go to the extreme of giving up their own well-being for them. Number 9 people have the ability to give unconditional love, much like a dog gives to his owner. Unconditional love is the closest to divine love. They can be very charitable and forgiving of others which makes them vulnerable to be taken advantage of. They tend to trust people too easily, which can create a large risk factor for them especially if someone plays on their emotional caring side. The words love and money vibrate to a 9 energy.

Number 9 is a very artistic energy, along with the 3 and 6. Many famous artists carry a 9 vibration in their blueprint. Number 9's are ultra-sensitive and are vulnerable and can be hurt very easily. They fear being alone and abandoned. They need a close connection to their own god/source energy to overcome that fear.

Number 9 is the number of completion when it comes to the temporary numbers. Crossing the finish line or bringing a meeting to a close. Number 9's can see many relationships come to an end in their lifetime. I always tell number 9's, "Do not rush into a relationship. Wait patiently until you can find someone that knows how to give unconditional love, like you do."

If you are a number 9 what purpose has your soul come to complete in this lifetime?

Number 9—Completion, love, artist, humanitarian, spiritual, compassionate, vulnerable, sensitive, feeling, unconditional love, service to others, lover, caring, nature lover, and animal lover.

Opposites

Vulnerable, fear of abandonment, stubborn, drama king or queen, nosy, holds a grudge, can't let go, trusting and serving others at your own expense, needs reassurance, lonely, needy.

Being an Overdone Number

Your blueprint in numerology has 8 different positions. If you have 3 or more positions with the same end number, you qualify as an overdone number of that digit.

When you are an overdone number, your overall personality is a little tilted in the energy direction of that number. It can feel like being on a see-saw and being weighed down to the ground on one side and not being able to lighten the load to get back to balance. All of your focus is drawn to that overdone number, whichever one it might be. It is advisable to work in the energy of your missing numbers whenever you can.

If you qualify as an overdone number, no matter which one it is, be aware of the warning signs so you don't do yourself or someone else a disservice that you will regret later. We all need to stay in balance, which means compensating for these overages. As an example:

An overdone number 1 will need to be the leader of the group and many times taking on more than they can handle. When that happens, everyone working under them gets the brunt of the overflow, which makes them a brute, being more demanding than is necessary.

An overdone number 2 is extra sensitive and intuitive, which might turn into overly sensitive to other people's energy and problems, and not have good enough boundaries to contain their own energy. When that happens the peaceful person that the number 2 is naturally can suddenly turn into an angry, miserable, critical, complaining and very unpleasant person to be around.

An overdone number 3 is the happy-go-lucky cheerleader type. When that exuberance gets overdone it can became giddy, loud, and talking over everyone. Or making everything a joke without taking anything seriously. They can be all play and never get the work done to succeed at anything because they are scattered. Their world is a chaotic mess. Chaos comes before creativity, but the overdone number 3 may never get to the creative part.

An overdone number 4 is the exact opposite of the overdone number 3. Their world is so structured that you cannot put down an item without it being picked up to be processed, cleaned, filed or thrown out if it does not fit into their plan. Of course they are also the workaholic who never takes time to play. Their priorities are very exact and adhered to. Strictness and disciple are law and order. They cannot go with the flow without falling apart at the seams.

Darlene Chadbourne

An overdone number 5 is easily addicted to something, because they are not grounding through themselves. They are trying to ground through a substance outside of themselves. Remember the number 5 wants to be a free spirit and does not like sitting still to focus on one task at a time. I am an overdone number 5. I have 3 number 5's in my 8 blueprint positions. It makes the task of writing this book a little difficult.

An overdone number 6 is such a caretaker of others that there is nothing left for the self—the ultimate in self-sacrifice, but then the person blames others for their lack of peace and harmony. They can be the mother hen who is the only one who knows how to do things right. It is their way or the highway when they get completely frazzled. They do not do the empty-nest syndrome very well, because they never took time to develop a life for themselves. They were too busy running the house, the family, the job, and now they don't know who they are without the responsibility for everyone else.

An overdone number 7 never has enough education—they want more and more information. Overdone number 7's are extremely spiritual; many seek the cloistered convent life or that of a priest or a minister, which can also cause others to think they are "holier than thou" and let you know it—the typical evangelist. Number 7's need lots of quiet alone time. The hermit describes them well.

An overdone number 8 is over-responsible, and feels that everything is their job to fix. They feel that they created every situation and they need to fix it. There is no rest for the number 8 person. If they don't have something to do every minute of every day they are bored. They are so good at multitasking that when nothing is happening it drives them crazy.

An overdone number 9 person is the humanitarian and people-pleaser who can have a fear of abandonment. They are always seeking unconditional love and will test people to find it.

One example is a person born in September, the 9th month, on the 9th day, in a year that totals a 27/9. When you add all those 9's together you get another nine. They are an overdone 9 energy. They can obsess over their ride being there on time.

Relationships are made more complex by the excessive number of 9's and the fear of abandonment.

Everyone with an overdone number situation has to work harder to balance out the other numbers that have no representation in their blueprint. It is similar to a potluck dinner, when everyone decides to bring the same thing.

Darlene Chadbourne

Mastery

You are here in this lifetime for a purpose. You need to find that purpose and to master it by taking the abilities that come with your numbers in your personal blueprint, and develop them to the master level of accomplishment. This is for everyone, not just those with master numbers.

If you do have one or more master numbers, your mission is more focused in the area of whatever that twin digit is. It is not as easy for you to vary your abilities across many numbers.

Knowing others is intelligence: knowing yourself is true wisdom.

Mastering others is strength, mastering yourself is true power.

Lao-Tzu, BC600-? Chinese Philosopher,

Founder of Taoism, Author of the "Tao Te Ching

To be one's own master is to be at liberty to act as one chooses, without dictation from anybody. Be a leader on your *path*, not a follower on someone else's *path*.

- Are you ready for a promotion in life?
- Are you ready to be promoted to Master of your life?

Master means being skilled at a certain task. You have to learn about the task and have specialized knowledge in order to become a master at it, i.e., Master Plumber, Master Sergeant. These usually mean having the means to fill the full potential of the job at hand.

Freedom Through Numbers

Being a master, or promoting yourself to master, means attaining the information that you need to fill the position or to ascend the ladder to elevate yourself to a higher level of consciousness. By raising your sails you can move from one place to another. If your sails are down on a ship, you either set your anchor to stay in one place, or you travel without direction whichever way the water and wind may flow.

Many of you have had your anchor in the same place for many years and have become stagnant in your existence. Others have been free flowing with no direction and not even knowing what tools you have available to you.

Becoming the master of your life is ascending to the position of full potential. Reaching your full potential requires you to use the tools for the job. You have each come equipped with the tools that you need to accomplish your mission in this lifetime.

Numerology is one of the many ancient tools that allows you to learn about what you have come equipped with and what you still have to gather in order to reach your full potential.

- The first step is to make the choice to master your life and live with purpose and intention, making the choice to set sail with a definite direction.
- The second step to mastery is knowing what tools you have to work with.
- The third step is knowing how to use those tools.

Darlene Chadbourne

- The fourth step is applying that knowledge to your own individual situation or station in life.

Master Numbers 11-99

*"In a real sense, every Master Number is the Soul
rising like a phoenix out of the limitations of its own base number."*
Korra Deaver, The Master Numbers in Numerology, p. 28

People with Master Numbers are defined by the twin digits 11 through 99. Their double digit amplifies the energy of the base number. All people with Master Numbers have come into this life with a humanitarian mission. The trick is to find out what that mission is. It is unique for every person. Master Numbers are here to be the humanitarians of the world, but not at their own expense. Being a master number is both a curse and a blessing. Many of my clients say, "I wish I had master numbers." And I say, " Be careful what you ask for." People with Master numbers usually come with a very heavy agenda, in order to get where they are going in this lifetime. Sometimes childhood can be more challenging as a Master Number, because the wisdom and knowing that comes naturally is not received well from a toddler or child. The parents don't know what to do with a child that knows things that they don't, so they convince the child that they are wrong or there is no such thing. The child then suppresses their knowing and doesn't share. It might take them half of their life to rediscover this closed-down piece of themselves that was denied expression when they were younger. In recent years it is more accepted that children can come in with gifts and talents that are inherent and not learned in this lifetime.

Master numbers are not easy to work with. Master numbers are different than the single digits and because of their complexity they require more work and focused attention. Master numbers are like going for a master's degree in a specific subject. It is taking a subject to the next level. Anyone can do this; it is taking what you are interested in to the next level. You may have never done it because you didn't know you could. No one told you that you could do anything that you set your mind to. No one gave you permission to try. You may have heard more of, "You can't do that. It is impossible."

The twin digits that create the master number determines the focused energy that needs to be mastered. This is not a small matter—the single digits are more straightforward. With a master number you have to focus more on the twin digit number in order to master its single digit. For example, the number 22/4 needs to work with understanding and developing relationships (2) in order to build (4) a business model that works.

To master means to make the commitment to being human in a deeper way. Like the master key will open all of the locks. As a master number, you have multiple aspects of yourself to open and use that you may or may not be aware of.

In thinking about how we arrive at a single digit in numerology, we start with the double or triple digit number and then reduce it by addition to a single digit. In most cases you have two or three different digits. Look at what these individual digits are in order to determine how you are going to accomplish the single digit. Take 42/6, for example. You would use the building material skills (4) in conjunction with another relationship (2) or person to accomplish the nurturer (6) that wants to support a family. This would describe two people working together to build a family, or a healing practice, or a table, or chair. If it is a 22/4, the person really has to figure out how to relate to others in order to build something. You have less energy numbers to provide assistance in attaining the single digit. So if the person doesn't master the 22 in relationships, he or she works with the 4 energy for his or her whole life. This makes this person feel incomplete and less accomplished.

With a master number you may have a more difficult path to complete the lesson of that number . You can always revert to the single digit, but don't shy away from it, because once attained the rewards are incredible. I am speaking from experience.

"All bearers of Master Numbers should make time to be alone frequently."
Korra Deaver, The Master Numbers in Numerology, p.23

Darlene Chadbourne

11/2 Master Psychic or Intuitive.

You bring wisdom from above and below into the heart chakra within, pulling this wisdom into the self, then you reiterate it outward to help others. You need to take the time to be quiet enough to hear, see, or know the information flowing into you through your personal access channel. By receiving visual images, hearing messages, knowing things that come to you, you feel the emotions of others. Reoccurring events that draw your attention are called synchronicities. This happens often to an 11/2 master number person. It is another way of receiving messages.

It is no coincidence that the words Wisdom (29/11/2), Wise (11/2), and Balance (11/2) all vibrate to 11/2.

It is your job to allow your psychic knowing to be a welcomed part of your life. You have a gift of knowing things that most people don't have. With this number you need to be aware of boundaries and be able to strengthen them so you are not being a sponge and picking up other peoples energy just by walking by.

The Bubble-Up exercise in the Tools chapter (p. 186) will work well for you.

22/4 The Master Builder.

You have the same psychic ability as the 11/2 but have a much easier time manifesting with it. There is an architectural energy to the 22/4 that needs to put things into material form. The double 2's are doubly sensitive to the feelings of others, which makes them want to be the peacemakers of the world. The 22/4 needs people in their life to help them build the connections to the people that have the next step and answers for continuing along their path. People are great resources for a 22/4 in building a better world.

33/6 is the Master Healer.

You are gifted in helping others, be it as a doctor or nurse, mother or teacher. There is a nurturing side to the 33 that seems to know exactly what the person needs for advancing their position in life. This could be in healing professions, childrearing, hospice, or feeding the masses. There seems to be a flow-through of information directing every step along the way for others. But many times you do not receive as easily as you give and end up sacrificing your own needs for others, as the Masters of Self-Sacrifice. You are born over-responsible for others and need to learn that you are one of humanity as well. You also need nurturing and loving aimed toward the self. You need to uplift yourself and soar while you are uplifting others. You need to accept that there are some situations that cannot be fixed and there comes a time to walk away, moving on to help someone else.

44/8 Master Therapist.

You are a good worker in the material world where hands-on is important. You are great at the exacting details required by some jobs. You discipline yourself to get the job done. Sometimes you won't quit until it is perfect. You buckle down and make yourself fit the situation, which is not always a good thing. When you can see concrete results, you feel like you are on top of the world. You need to have your work be useful, and better yet, helping humanity in a philanthropic way. You are always for the underdog as long as they want to do the work it takes to help themselves. I have heard it said that a 44/8 can make a million dollars, lose a million and make another million. Being the Master Therapist, you need to release your own baggage while you are helping others.

I found a perfect statement for the 44/8 today in James Wanless' *Way of the Great Oracle, the Voyager Tarot*, under the card titled "Confusion", p. 219.

"Brainstorm. Allow the creative chaos of competing ideas and points of view. Do not censor anything. In this state of extreme mental activity and agitation, great ideas are born.....
Think with an open mind. Investigate all possibilities. Only by knowing the parameters can you intelligently know your values and make your decisions."

Darlene Chadbourne

The energy of the word Confusion is a 44/8. Then the word Parameters caught my attention. It is also a 44/8. So this says to me that when you are in confusion you need to push things out to the edges of your parameters of thinking or create new parameters in order to make a decision. As a 44/8 you have broader parameters then most people so you have more to deal with and more to choose from. Your choices are unlimited. The word Unlimited is a 44/8. When you try to limit yourself to narrow parameters or resist all of the ideas and information, you close the mind down.

> *"In keeping your mind and beliefs in check, you suffer headaches and loss of energy and/or you engage in unhealthy behavior to relax the mind."*
> Ibid, p.220

55/10/1 Master Intellectual or Master Teacher.

      The 55 signifies the intellectual aspect of life, and then as it reduces down to a 10, it signifies leadership and guidance, equating to the teacher. The 55 person has great curiosity and loves to explore and travel the world. The 55 can also master other languages with more ease than most. You are a lover of the written word, which can also make you a talented writer. You can become an outstanding explorer or researcher with the need to know that drives your curiosity. You can be extreme in taking things to the ultimate edge and pursuing your ideas with great intensity that might make others uncomfortable. You want law and order as long as it supports your way of thinking how things should be. This leads to mercy and justice on your terms. You have a difficult time seeing both sides of an issue, so tread lightly with power over others, which is the down side of the number 1 energy.

66/12/3 Master Cosmic Parent.

You are caring and responsible for others, which makes you a great mother or father. You live by your ideals of beauty and harmony. You love the comfort of a peaceful and happy home life. You will pursue your concepts for bettering our social and natural environments. You are very practical in your abilities to see the source of a problem and to come up with very practical solutions. People are attracted to you for your talents and accomplishments. You are very generous in helping the underdog or those in difficult times. You love growing things, be it children and family, a garden, or money for a cause.

77/14/5 Master Philosopher. (The master numbers 77 through 99 are very rare.)

"This is a lifetime for spiritualizing the material and materializing the spiritual."

Korra Deaver, The Master Numbers in Numerology, p. 93

You seek perfection in all endeavors. You may receive good fortune through surprising ways, like something out of nothing, or so it appears. It may seem magical at times through unexpected inheritances or gifts from unexpected places. You attain a comfort in life that allows you to rest and be meditative, which feeds your soul and is necessary to your well-being. You have the ability to see deeply into other peoples' situations, and you bring forth great compassion and understanding to help others. This ability draws an incredible amount of gratitude from the people that you help. It can be as little as a simple smile that allows people to recognize the ray of sunshine that you bring into a situation. You show up and do whatever needs to be done to improve a situation. People love to have you involved in their life. You are emotionally very stable no matter what the situation calls for. Your imagination and creativity are a direct result of your incredible sense of knowing what to do when, especially for others. You are very sensitive to other people's needs, which can also be overwhelming at times. The Bubble-Up exercise in the Appendix (p. 186) is very helpful.

Darlene Chadbourne

88/16/7 Master of Business Management. This can lead to being a Master of Success, especially concerning the flow of money. It makes me think of flow charts and waterfalls, both with infinite sources. You need to think large, more like global in scope. You do not do well being contained or confined. You need unlimited thought and concepts of world-wide expansion as you bring your spiritual knowing to task, while operating in the material world of commodities and financial endeavors. You think in humanitarian terms of philanthropy at the global level with the creative ideas that can make things manifest. The multitasker in you needs to be the boss and not the employee. The head of a large corporation or self-made millionaire is not beyond your reach. As the boss you can recognize the potential in others to help them succeed as well, bringing them up the ladder with you. You want to see them learn how to feel the accomplishment of a job well done. You are very easily admired by others who try to follow your lead. Like the single number 8 you can make a million and lose a million and make another million.

99/18/9 Master Humanitarian. This master number reminds me of the song, "*What the World Needs Now is Love Sweet Love.*" You are the humanitarian that wants everyone to know the feeling of unconditional love. You want the global human scene operating like a well-oiled machine with all of the gears intermeshed and running smoothly, with everyone getting along with everyone else in the ideal situation of cooperation and efficiency that can produce the best results for each and every human being on this earth at this time. You find yourself seeking out and mixing with people of importance that can make things happen, and have the means to do so. You use the media to get the word out, sponsoring global events to draw attention to the cause for the masses. You have no trouble getting up on stage and teaching love and compassion from everyone for everyone. You are all-inclusive and have no threads of prejudice within you. You are altruistic with a charisma that can sell anything good or bad. Your intentions need to be genuine, for the good of all, from a much higher source of perfection than we have ever attained so far in our history on this planet.

An Overdone Master Number

I have mentioned overdone numbers referring to the single-digit numbers in a previous section. This section is about overdone master numbers, which would be three or more master numbers in a person's blueprint. In this case, they do not have to be identical master numbers, they can be any of the master numbers from 11 to 99.

It used to be that master numbers were more rare because of the rule of reducing everything to a single digit. In my Native Path Method, I specifically use the whole equation so I do not miss any of the hidden master numbers or zeros.

An overdone master number person with three or more master numbers has a tendency to be more sensitive both spiritually and emotionally. There is a website devoted to the subject of highly sensitive people. (HSP). This population started appearing in the early 1990's. In some spiritual circles they were called the Indigo Children. This population of highly sensitive people with overdone master numbers may choose to not be in the world, but retreat from society, unable to cope with the pressures and expectations. It may make it difficult for them to sort out life's simplest challenges at times. This may be caused by their lack of boundaries and how to sort out what is theirs and what belongs to other people they may encounter. Therefore they seldom feel safe enough to allow their true colors or their soul's essence to shine out in its full magnificence.

The parents of such HSP children have their job cut out for them. It will not be easy to raise their child through the rough years of growing up without squelching their unique and sensitive soul essence. Support and teach them to believe in themselves, when they don't feel like they fit in this world. The parent also does not want them to develop a false sense of ego. They will need to get them to understand and forgive others, yet still hold on to their own self-worth.

All master numbers, especially overdone master numbers, need to spend time alone to give the mind a rest from being on guard. This is the easiest way they can find to create the peace and tranquility they need to feel safe enough to fit in.

If you are a supportive parent of who they are as individuals and allow them to express themselves according to their individual path in life, they will be fine. It is the older generations that thought children were to be seen but not heard. The parents would tell them that there is no such thing as seeing spirits or imaginary friends in their room. Spirituality was not accepted, so anyone coming in as a master number would hit the ground running and want to do their purpose, helping everyone in their life. But the parents would suppress them and their natural soul's desire—but most of all they would discount their intuition. Then a person would have to get to midlife to uncover the suppression and get back to their true self.

Darlene Chadbourne

The most recent generation of Indigo Children are now parents. They are more intuitive themselves, and accept it and understand it as a part of who we naturally are.

Darlene Chadbourne

Chapter 4
Time Cycles

Working your Numbers, Timing is Everything

According to numerology we live in 9 year epicycles.

Now it is time to calculate your personal year to see what temporary number you are in this year. Are you in the beginning, the middle, or the end of the numbers 1 to 9?

Personal Epicycle (Month + Day + Current Year = Personal Year)

Your Last Birthday: PERSONAL YEAR

Your month + day of birth + current year = your personal year or Epicycle number. Calculate temporary numbers similar to the date of birth for the Native Path, but in this case use the current year instead of the birth year.

- Total of four digits of the Current Year = the Universal Year Energy for all of Earth.
- Birth Month + Birth Day + Current Year = Personal Year Energy for you.

Freedom Through Numbers

Temporary Numbers and Timing

Timing has to do with the temporary numbers. The timing numbers place you in the space and time of the universal time clock. When synchronicity comes into play, your personal numbers are in synch with your blueprint numbers.

These are points in time when things are activated and windows of opportunity are opened for you. Not for everyone, but for you personally, according to your personal blueprint, your positions, and your timing in the grand scheme of things.

These temporary numbers are what activates your blueprint and puts your blueprint into motion. This is called working your numbers, and is the step that takes your knowledge beyond knowing your numbers. "*TIMING IS EVERYTHING*" is the cliché that works in the temporary numbers section of your annual updated blueprint.

Your temporary numbers can be stated for the year, the month, the day, the hour, and the minute if need be. I genuinely give thanks and gratitude to Faith Javane and Dusty Bunker for their book, *Numerology and the Divine Triangle*. This is where I found the process for the timing of the trimesters dividing the year into three—four-month periods. This is a very important part of the temporary chart. These trimesters are the perfect length of time to work with when you are attempting to create change and development in your life. This is where you look to make progress and create step-by-step plans. A year is too long and a month is too short, but a trimester is perfect for creating and implementing change. This trimester of time gives you the time for research and development. We all know that day-to-day living takes time. There will always be the need for sleep, food prep, eating and cleaning.

I find that in my mentoring entrepreneurs, this is the most useful and practical application of your personal blueprint and the blueprint of an entrepreneur's business. It produces the best results. Many come back and say, "It happened right during that trimester that you said it might, the way you said was possible during that time frame when it matched one of my blueprint numbers."

Looking at these time frames sets up a chance for synchronicity to work because you are aligning your intentions and focus with your universal time clock. This is the one your soul chose when it came into this earth plane, to specifically chosen parents that would set you up to accomplish your mission, purpose, and self-importance to experience your freedom right now.

Think of numerology as a giant puzzle of your life with all the individual pieces that need to be identified by number, by place, by tense, by timing in order to put it together to see the bigger picture. This shines the lights, camera, and action on your life.

You are then stepping in to be not only the producer, but also the director, cameraman, editor, and the creator of your own life by living it to the fullest with passion, purpose, and potential, *FREE* to be you.

Freedom Through Numbers

The Decades

    The importance of Decades come from the 0 which is within every decade marker. The changing of the decade is like the changing of the guard. The Zero signifies a change in time increments.

    The Zero opens up the energy to spiritual re-patterning. It is the marker between the decades that signifies the advancement to the next level of existence on the Earth plane. This opens you up to a new slate of possibilities if you invite it in and allow yourself to advance your energy to the next level.

What Decade Were You Born In?

The decades we are born in define soul groups that come in to a certain period of time to create a societal change. There will be a theme dependent on the vibration of numbers.

1910-1919 Were born into this world to work on a sense of identity of the Self(1).

1920-1929 Were born into this world to work on cooperation and teamwork(2).

1930-1939 Were born into the world to work on Communication skills(3).

1940-1949 Were born into this world to work on new foundations and structures(4).

1950-1959 The beginnings of change and awareness of outer planetary energies—expanding the boundaries of society's thinking and scope of awareness(5).

1960-1969 The window of Aquarius and preparing for the new millennium(6).

1970-1979 The opening up of Spirituality and alternative healing modalities(7).

1980-1989 A huge expansion of awareness of the connection of above and below(8).

1990-1999 Lots of culminations and completions and more focus on humanitarian concerns. The Indigo Children are born with special awareness(9).

2000-2009 The beginning of the spiritual awareness of the new millennium. Those who are here to change the world as we know it(0). Since 2001 is the only year with a 1, limited attention is given to the self. It is mostly about others (2) for the whole century.

2010-2019 The number 1 is back as part of the year number, but only for this decade(1). After this it will only appear in the year number once every 10 years.

2020-2029 The doubles 2's create a new sense of relationships. The phrase "Diversity into Unity" is the theme going forward into the Age of Aquarius.

Darlene Chadbourne
~ 130 ~

What Decade is Your Age in Now?

Age

0-9 The soul comes into the body and must figure out how to fulfill its purpose while in the confines of a body.

10-19 You are trying to define who you are as an individual.

20-29 Relating to others in all types of relationships: personal, work-related, intimate, and as child or a parent.

30-39 Communication is the key in your 30s, as well as creativity. I notice more of this current generation is waiting until their 30s to have children.

40-49 This time in your life is about creating a new solid foundation for yourself, different from the one your parents supplied for you to grow up on. This is a big part of the mid-life crisis phase that people go through. What do I want?

50-59 This is a time to create the changes that build the new structure on that foundation you built in your 40s.

60-69 This is the time to develop harmony and balance to allow you to enjoy the rest of your life.

70-79 This is the time of focusing on spirituality and how your life fits into the overall population as a part of the oneness of all.

80-89 This is the time to be the connecting rod between Heaven and Earth in a more dedicated and purposeful life of helping others.

90-99 This is the ultimate humanitarian energy that brings about thoughts of completions and accomplishments, as in taking inventory of what you have done and what you still want to do while in a physical body.

100-110 I would imagine that this decade would bring you back to the joy, innocence and freedom of accomplishment and no responsibilities to others.

Chapter 5

Name Changes

Nothing overrides your original birth name and date of birth. However, circumstances sometimes call for changing your name. The only time it signifies creating a second blueprint is when it is done legally, with the date that it transpires, making it a legal document just like your birth certificate.

Legal Name Change as an Adult

There are times when an adult finds reasons to change their name legally.

I have had clients who had a spiritual awakening which then prompted them to change their name to something more fitting. There have been clients that have changed their name for recognition and fame, which is more like a stage name. It is important to do the blueprint for these, because they might stick for a lifetime, and almost nobody knows them by their birth name. The same applies to a pen name of an author.

It does not apply to a nickname that is applied without a legal document.

Name Change through Marriage

Women or men who change their surname to their spouse's last name through a legal document like a *marriage certificate*, qualifies for a new Blueprint. The original Birth name and date still apply for the major blueprint. The *marriage certificate* is considered a minor name vibration, significant mainly if used for signatures. It still does not override the birth certificate name Blueprint. This usually happens in your 20's or 30's, or later after you have already lived your life under your birth name for a few decades or more. The Blueprint for your *married* name is considered a *minor* influence.

Name Change for Adoptions

Create second Blueprint using the court documents of the adoption with the *legal date* and *new name* (refer to the following Chapter on Adoption).

Chapter 6

Adoption

Please note that all adoptees in my opinion are very old souls with a big job to do in touching many people's lives through many families. It is not about being wanted or not wanted, it is about how many people you can touch in this lifetime. You are here to make a difference in many peoples' lives. I feel that these are soul contracts that you made before you came into a physical body.

Do not be surprised that you have to work on the lessons of loss and abandonment and lots of change. This is very normal for an adoptee. These are heavy-duty lessons to take seriously. The biggest gift you can give to yourself is self-love and acceptance.

If you are an adoptee, gather as much information as possible from your time of birth, *Date/Time/Name* on original *Birth Certificate* if possible. Many of the agencies are able to release that information now, especially to you the adult.

Double Blueprints

You will always run two blueprints for adoptees—one with the birth information, even if it is *Baby Boy* or *Baby Girl*. Or maybe *Baby* with a last name only.

And the second with the court documents for the adoption with the date and new name. I find in my experiences with my granddaughters and clients that they either have many crossover numbers that are the same between the two blueprints, or if they are quite different, then they use traits and habits, gifts and passions from both blueprints.

Think if you were in a poker or bridge game and instead of being dealt one hand you were dealt two hands and you were able to pick and choose from either hand. That is what it is like when you have been adopted and have two blueprints to work with.

The only other thing to consider when you are adopted is the location of where you started your life.

Roots and Adoption

It is very helpful to calculate the energy of your *birth place City, State*, and sometimes *Country* if different from where you are now. Next, your current location *City* and *State,* then match them to your blueprint numbers.

This is especially necessary for adoptees who are removed from the continent that they were born on. I believe that the soul chooses its parents and location to enter the Earth plane

Let's use the example of being born in China and then ending up in the United States.

Do the numerology of both countries. Remember to use the whole name,

United States of America = 84/12/3. USA = 5.

People's Republic of China = 103/4 or 103/22/4. China = 26/8.

Match the numbers to your blueprint numbers.

It is particularly strong if it matches your soul number. Only the single end number in each equation needs to match.

The Importance of Roots

Roots are your connection point to the Earth energy. This is your first point of reference for experiencing your lifetime. The location is important to your landing in a physical body. The energy of that location resides in your cellular memory. You could have a feeling that you are missing something and spend your whole life searching for what is missing. If this sounds like something you experience, go back to the place of your birth, either in person or telepathically for the purpose of pulling up your roots and replanting them where you currently live.

Correlate this to transplanting a house plant or a seedling into a garden. You would not cut off the plant and leave the roots behind. This is the same concept, in an energetic sense. Considering the roots of your origin is even more significant in cases of adoption from another country. Or even the separation from the mother for a long time after birth, due to illness of the mother or the baby. With these two situations, the connection is lost with the mother and possibly the father, as well as the connection to the earth if the baby is transported out of the area, or the country, or the continent. The connection to the location and roots of your birth may also be disturbed in children whose families move often, like in a military family who is reassigned often. The soul has reasons for choosing the parents to whom they are born, but all of a sudden the soul's plans are overridden by circumstances out of its control or the parents' control.

Darlene Chadbourne

In the case of adoptees, there is a double disconnect: separation from the mother and father and separation from the location of the place of birth. Reclaiming the missing energies from your early life when you were not old enough to make your own choices is vitally important.

These broken connections are more traumatic in childhood and the residue is carried a lifetime. You will never feel like you are complete if the connection is not consciously reclaimed and reconnected, even if it is only in an energetic intention on your part. The most important starting point is to know that something is missing before you can find and reclaim it. This is not about blaming anyone for these circumstances. It is about healing the missing energetic connection.

Roots and Location

It is very important to know where you have come from, before you can know where you are in the present and where you want to go in the future. I don't feel that we give enough importance to place.

I do many location readings for people who have to move due to jobs or due to choice in locations. This is where I ask them to look at the general area they plan on moving to. Then they create a list of not more than 10 places that they would like to be, in that area. This list includes the full street address (if known at this point), the city, the state, and the country if it means crossing a border. I then calculate the numbers for each of those items and compare them to the person or persons' Blueprints to find the most compatible place for them to be out of those 10 locations. This could be a multiple-step process.

Try this yourself. Calculate your street address, city and state and see if you have any matches to your blueprint numbers. Use the same method for calculating that you used for your name.

Darlene Chadbourne

Part Two

Chapter 7

Finding Your "I AM"

Why "I am that I am" and the 3-circle diagram is so important to me.

The moment that this came together was bigger than an "aha" moment. I think we all have "aha" moments once in awhile. But this moment was bigger than that and that is why it is so hard to describe.

I was attending college at the time, back in 1998. It was my dreaded Math component study that I had been putting off since I started college in 1995. My professor for this study said, "I think you need this book. I am going to loan it to you because it is out of print." The name of the book is *Time Stands Still,* by Keith Critchlow, an architect. He was explaining the sacred geometry of buildings on sacred sites and universal concepts that had to do with geometry.

I read the book and nothing much happened. That all changed when I had to write to the professor about the book and describe how it affected my life.

I still don't know what hit me that day. It was like a four-drawer file cabinet was opened up and everything in it was dumped on the floor. Then everything from the floor came into my head and lined up perfectly for a very clear understanding of a concept that I had never realized before.

My original concept of that understanding is shown on p. 143. In my eyes it describes the divide and conquer mentality of the patriarchy during the Piscean Age that we have been living under for two thousand-plus years.

No more power over others!

The second diagram blew my mind with the three circles overlapping and working together (p. 144). This describes the Age of Aquarius that we will be in for the next two thousand plus years. Realizing your own internal power for relationships where unity and diversity come together.

Now it is about power from within each individual.

Darlene Chadbourne

Heaven

Earth

Freedom Through Numbers
~ 143 ~

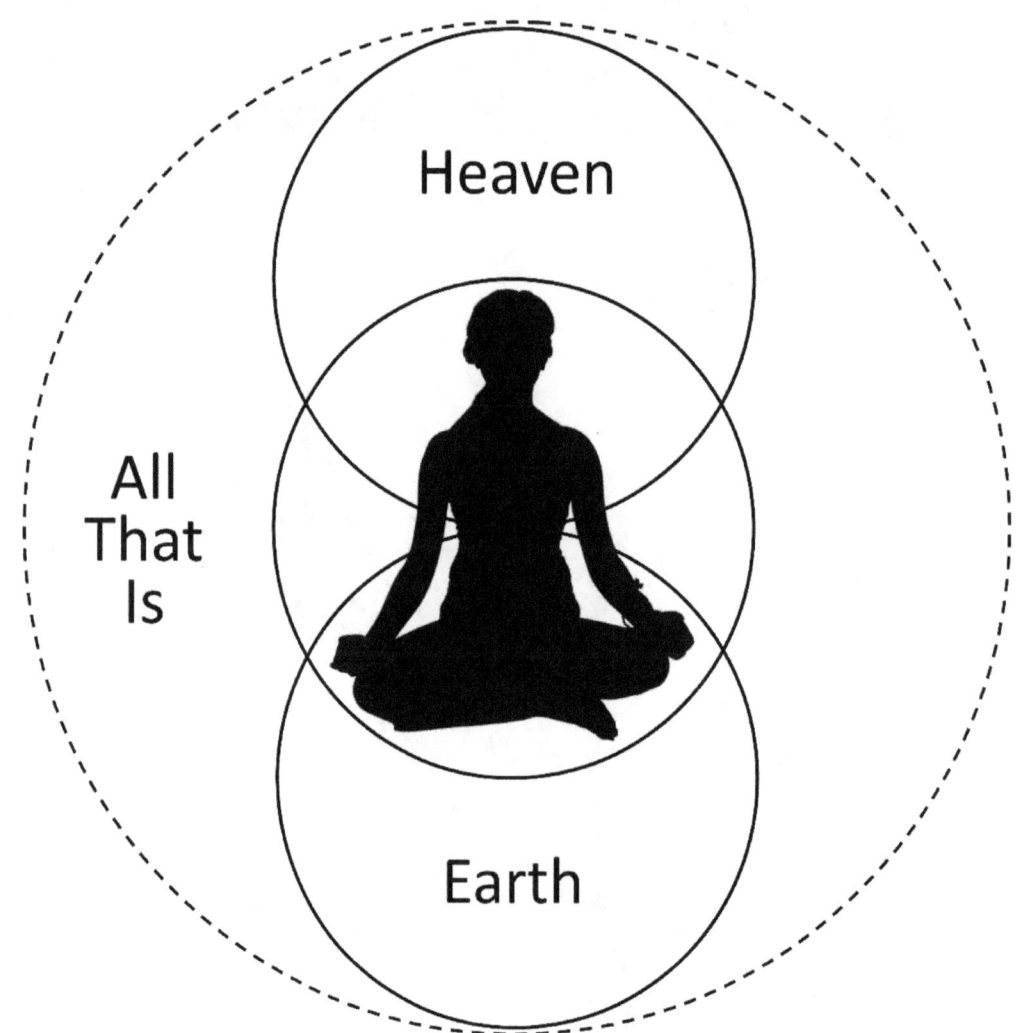

Darlene Chadbourne

The whole thing was about these three circles being one over the other, in my mind. The top one was labeled as heaven, middle as mankind, and bottom as earth. In the book, those same three circles were overlapped, as in one over the other to create an almond-shaped vesica-pisces. So all three of them were connected. The center circle of mankind showed a diagram of a person sitting in a yogi/Buddha position, with their crown chakra (top of head) touching the center of heaven and their root chakra (tail bone) touching the center of the earth circle.

All of a sudden I understood the concept of mankind (me) being the connecting rod between heaven and Earth. I had heard for years that it is our job to make heaven on Earth. I never knew what that meant. I was raised Catholic, and heaven was always up there someplace and you had to die to get there. And we didn't pay attention to the Earth. All of a sudden that three-circle interlocking diagram took on a new meaning for me. It just blew my mind. With that realization sinking in, I came out of my office. I was laughing, I was crying, I was giggling. I couldn't talk. I didn't know what was happening. My daughter was in the kitchen and she didn't know what to do with me. All she did was keep looking at me. She said I went on and on and on. It was like babble was coming out of me. My guess is that I was excited about this conclusion I had come to. I wondered, how do I write that to my professor?

A moment beyond words where my daughter thought I had gone crazy. An awareness like I had never had before.

Freedom Through Numbers

Something deeper happened when I had that vision or awareness that these are all supposed to be connected: Then came the realization, fast and furious once I saw the drawing, the sacred geometry made sense. First the *Figure 8 Exercise* (p. 156), then the *I AM Mantra* (p. 157); followed by the drawing on the front cover with the connection to the merkaba and the tree came flowing out of me.

That is why this "I am that I am" diagram is so powerful for me.

This understanding changed me in a way that I couldn't even believe, if I just got out of the way and allowed things to happen. It is that awareness that allowed me to write the "I AM" Mantra (p. 157).

Once I found my "I AM" and my connection to *All That Is*, I realized a self-propelled power within me that I had never experienced before. I felt that I was plugged into a power source that was not available to me earlier. I had found an identity of self-importance, not just an identity as the caretaker of others. Previously I identified as just one of the herd with no knowing, want or desire for what my individual purpose and power was. This was the first time I had a want that I could identify as mine, like I mentioned in the beginning of this book. This power was like a light that was never there before. Like the light at the end of the tunnel in the *Tunnel* story in Part One (p. 23).

I am realizing that this is about light and my own enlightenment. I have moved out of the darkness of the herd mentality. Once only a single spark, I turned into a flame as in the *Cold Pot Belly* poem. (p. 33) My whole transformation has been about turning on and plugging into my own power source and making the connections for my personal passion, purpose, and potential.

    I see it as we are all like a lamp when we are born. It is like buying a lamp at the store, bringing it home and setting it on the table. Then, you expect light to emanate from it. After all, it is a lamp. No one said that a few connections had to be made before I could get light out of the lamp.

Above	I had to buy a light bulb to insert in the top of the lamp.	Heaven
	Even with the light bulb in the lamp. I did not get any light.	
Middle	The lamp You are the lamp.	Yourself
Below	I had to take the end of the cord and plug it into	Earth
	a grounded outlet. Grounded to the Earth below.	
	Plugging it in without a light bulb, I did not get any light.	

    All three need to be connected: The Bulb, The Lamp, The Grounded, Plugged-in Cord.

    When all three items were connected. I got light from the lamp. You are the lamp and you need the connection to *All That Is,* above, and to *Earth*, below, to enlighten and illuminate your personal "I AM." Only when all three are connected can you be an empowered individual.

Your "I AM" is your power source. Get connected by referring to the Figure 8 Exercise (p. 156) and the "I AM" Mantra (p. 157).
Getting out of the way, allowing, and trusting is your way to manifestation.
The next step is in the power of words and building affirmations that match your blueprint numbers. Continue reading to pull together the intentional energy of affirmations.

Manifesting: Name It, Claim It, Become It

There have been many great observers of life, like Pythagoras, Leonardo DaVinci, and Jung, who have changed the world, simply by paying attention and observing what is going on around them and within them.

Be the observer first, then be the change. Create the world the way you want to see it. You have to see it first, believe it second, and become it third. Or name it, claim it, and then become it. Become the observer, then the creator of your world.

Numerology is a very easy-to-use tool to help you get to know yourself and the potential you have available to you. Numerology is a way to look at and observe yourself in depth so you can discover and apply the Naming, Claiming, and Becoming of the Native Path method.

My purpose in writing this book is to facilitate your personal process in:

- Birthing your complete "I AM" presence;
- Building your self-confident "I AM";
- Becoming your total "I AM".

Defining the "I AM"

We have spent a whole eon of time detached from our personal source of power, the "I AM." Your "I AM," as I am using it here, is your personal power source.

You are an energetic being with an energy field. You may be oblivious to the source of power available to you. Oh! if you knew how to plug into that personal power source! You may have been brought up thinking you have to go through something or someone else to get fully empowered.

You can use the power of intention and thought to plug in and turn on your own dynamic energy source. The connection, when activated, is called the "I AM." As in the biblical text, when God spoke to Moses in the story of the Burning Bush, "I AM That I AM." When you allow yourself to be the connecting rod between Heaven and Earth you activate an energy source that flows like the number 8. The number 8 is the only number that has continuous motion, tracing around and around. Your Kundalini is an energy line from your root chakra to your crown chakra and represents your number 1 of the self. Your crown chakra connects you to the center of the heavens or All That Is. Your root chakra connects you to the crystal core of the center of the Earth.

Picture the diagram of a person sitting in a Buddha pose or yoga pose with the crown chakra connecting to the center of heaven and All That Is. Then picture your root chakra connected to the very crystal core of the Earth with the Kundalini line.

Darlene Chadbourne

"I AM"—such powerful letters when combined.

> I is a number 9 which is about completion, wholeness, and unconditional Love.
>
> A is a number 1 which is about the self and personal leadership.
>
> M is a number 4 which is about the Earth and material things.
>
> 9 + 1 + 4 = 14   1 + 4 = 5
>
> The total of the three digits is 14. When the 14 is reduced it is a number 5 and is written as 14/5.
>
> The number 5 is the number of freedom of the spirit to soar.
>
> The number 5 is the language of communication through the written word.
>
> The phrase "I AM That, I AM" is also 14/5, the Self (1) grounded (4) in the

above and below, which gives you the power (32/5) to change.

> Here are some sample Affirmations for the number 1.

Sample Affirmations:

I have chosen one word from each of the columns that reduce to a 1.

I AM fast (10/1)

I AM sexy (19/10/1)

I AM focused (28/10/1)

I AM assertive (37/10/1)

Freedom Through Numbers

I AM wonderful (46/10/1)

I AM intelligent (55/10/1)

You get the idea. You can do this for every one of your Blueprint positions.

The Power of Thoughts and Words

Every word vibrates and has an energy, such as:

    Birthing 51/6

    Building 42/6

    Becoming 41/5

    Naming 31/4

    Claiming 32/5

    Becoming 41/5

    Total of Naming, Claiming, and Becoming together is 14/5.

    Total of Naming, Claiming, Becoming, and "I AM" is 28/10/1.

The number 6 of both Birthing and Building is about *balance, harmony*, and *healing*. The number 5 of both Becoming and Claiming is about change and freedom. The number 4 of Naming is about building a structure in the material world and being very grounded. The 28/10/1 is about working together, number 2, with the above and below, number 8; 10/1 is a new beginning (1) with an uplifting of spirit (0).

Freedom Through Numbers

The Power of the "I AM"

This is the power of connection. When the "I AM" is activated through connection, your power increases tenfold. By following the exercise and the mantra on the following page every day, you will be renewing and reinforcing that power source. You will be plugging into your light source.

Find the True Authentic You

Freedom Through Numbers

Figure 8 "I AM" Exercise:

- Bend over, touching the ground if possible, or as close as you can get.
- Spread your arms to the sides.
- Scoop up the Earth's energy, bringing it to your heart, in a crossing-your-heart motion.
- Spread your hands out to the sides.
- Reach up over your head.
- Scoop down the Heavenly energy, bringing it to your heart, in a crossing-your-heart motion.
- Repeat 3 times (5 times if working with others that day).
- Feel the energy coursing through your body.
- Finish with your hands together in prayer position and say:

The "I AM" Mantra

I am fully connected above and below,
my job today is to just show up.
God, Universe, Spirit, your job
is to bring me safely to where I need to be.
Bring to me who needs to see me
and bring me to whomever I need to see
to fulfill my purpose in this lifetime.
Copyright © 2000, Darlene Chadbourne

(The following is a note to your higher self or soul self, or your "I AM").

NO STRINGS ATTACHED

I love you

  You are so special to me.

    You are so real.

      You wear no masks.

        You do not pretend.

          You feel so true.

            You are pure love.

I love you

  You love me for who I am.

    You allow me to be real.

      You love me with no strings attached.

        You have no expectations of me.

          You have always been there for me when I needed you.

I love you

  You and I bonded right after I arrived.

    You rescued me in those early years.

      You were my only example of normal.

        You were a safe haven for me.

Darlene Chadbourne

You gave me space to be away from the chaos and confusion.

You gave me security when I had none.

I love you

Our bond has lasted a lifetime.

Our bond has survived the distance.

Our bond is at a soul level.

Our bond was there before I was born.

Our bond will be there after we die.

Our bond is the God within us.

Our bond is that of two spirits allowing each other to be free.

I love you

True pure love is unconditional, under all conditions, no strings attached.

Thank you for being my unconditional lover all these years.

Thank you for your example of pure unconditional love.

Thank you for being an angel in my life.

I love you

(You also could use this as a meditation.)

Freedom Through Numbers

Darlene Chadbourne

Chapter 8

Be the Star that You Are:
If You Can't Hide It, Feature It

A friend once told me, "If you can't fix it, feature it." I also like to say, "If you can't hide it, feature it." Either way, you are meant to feature who you are. Most of us think we need fixing in one way or another, so we don't put ourselves out there.

Do you try to hide the gems and jewels of who you really are? These gems and jewels are the gifts and talents you were born with. Sometimes you know what these are; sometimes you need to do a little excavating to find them. Usually they are outstanding and need a spotlight shined on them. But that might be contradictory to what you have been told.

The following are specific to certain generations that you may or may not relate to:

"Don't be too big for your britches."

"Don't think you are better than others."

"Don't be a show-off."

"People don't like a show-off."

Of course this was done to prevent the opposite of ego—arrogance, and obnoxious false ego.

Finding and promoting a healthy ego, is what is necessary. In this day and age, children now are pushed to be all that they can be and to be proud of who they are.

Finding the middle ground is your self-importance. Rating scales run from 1 the lowest to 10 the highest. Where is your self-esteem on the scale? If it is not a 10, what will it take to get it there? Now this is not measured by someone else's standards but by your standards. Finding your personal 10/1 *self-importance* is most important to your well-being. Give yourself permission to stand tall in your *self-importance*.

My definition of *self-importance*: It is not *ego* or *arrogance*, "it is acknowledging that you were born into this life for a purpose and you intend to fulfill your purpose in this lifetime."

Your personal blueprint numbers are like a lens that you can use to see and live your life through. You are a complex being, having a combination of multiple lenses that make up your whole persona. Each of us has specialties of things that come easy to us. And challenges of things that take effort to conquer and enhance to make it part of the whole of who you are. These challenges, when known and recognized, need to be honored. Look at the big picture of who you are, as a whole, then break it down into the smaller pieces of step-by-step plans to work on the details.

Sometimes you might try to do it all by yourself, to be the multi-tasking super hero. Unless you are a strong 8 energy, learn to delegate some of those details to others. The word *delegate* vibrates to a 32/5 energy.

Darlene Chadbourne

Here is a break-down of what the number equation for *delegate* means: Communication is the (3) + with others is the (2) = be a free spirit and to create change (5). Together they are a number (5). *Delegating* is a skill worth learning.

Were you brought up with the concept that you had to do it all on your own? If you could not do it all by yourself, there was something wrong with you. This belief opens the door for shame and blame to come in and reinforce the fact that you were not good enough to get the job done; so you had to work hard and strive to know more and be more. This belief confined you to a self-imposed labor camp of try harder, work harder, do more, be better. Because you are never good enough, if you can't do it all.

What if you have spent all of your time trying to do what was not yours to do? What if you confined yourself to a life-sentence of doing what others told you to do, rather than what you wanted to do, and had a passion for? What if someone pointed out what was yours to do and then gave you permission to specialize in doing what you loved to do? Would that remove the life sentence and give you the FREEDOM you are looking for? Numerology does that!

Knowing your numbers is one thing, familiarizing yourself with each of your numbers as a lens and learning how to use it to look at your world through that lens is another. There are the numbers 1-9 and then there is "0" as in "Spirit has your back." Or are you one who struggles with the master numbers, all those twin digits from 11/2 to 99/18/9?

The next step is, knowing your Blueprint positions or the rooms in your personalized house of where each of the numbers resides in your life. These Blueprint positions also help to determine the time frame of when the numbers need to be activated or when they need to be kept in reserve for future use.

Each position has a past, present, or future tense to it, much like our correct use of tense in our sentence structure in grammar. Diagramming a sentence correctly and diagramming your life through numerology have similarities.

Turn on Your Light for the World to See

Naming, Claiming, & Becoming Your Full Number Blueprint & Potential

This book is about the process of working your personal Blueprint numbers through the power of words. *Love* and *fear* cannot live in the same place.

You have learned how to figure your 8 personal Blueprint numbers from your date of birth and your full name at birth.

You will discover how to enhance your "I AM" presence to full power with the exercises and words to represent each of your personal numbers. You will find words from the word list or your own vocabulary that express each of your personal numbers for you. What would that sound like?

You will create an "I AM" affirmative statement for each of your numbers with the words you have chosen. For example, "I AM competent." Competent vibrates to a number 3 energy.

You will apply the visual by finding pictures or items that express each of those numbers for you. Create a collage, two-dimensional (with pictures) or three-dimensional (with objects, such as an altar). What would that look like?

Next, combine all of your number collages into a story board/collage of your total package. When you see your full potential in the visual, you will have the model of you living your full potential.

Use this book as an interactive tool to see your full potential as your full gift to the world.

Continue by applying your numbers to the *Merkaba*, which is a three-dimensional 6-pointed star. Then apply the Merkaba to the three-circle theory, with *Mer* as Light, *Ka* as Spirit, and *Ba* as Body, to entwine the numbers with the "I AM" Presence.

By doing the exercises and mantra you will empower yourself to make a difference in the world.

This book will help you to change the image of who you are into becoming and being, a full present (as in gift) to the world. We are all here for a reason, and this book helps you to define your reason for being here.

Destiny, Inner Guidance, and Soul number come from the heavens above in the triangle that is pointing down, forming the image of a cup, feminine energy. Maturity, Native Path, and Personality come from Earth below in the triangle that is pointing up, forming the phallic symbol, masculine energy.

Darlene Chadbourne

It is when the masculine and feminine are in equal overlapping balance that it forms the merkaba shape. The merkaba in 2-D forms a Star of David, 6-pointed star. In 3-D it forms the merkaba. With the 3-D merkaba you can place the career/success number in the center on the point that is protruding. This shows that joining the above and below allows you to accomplish your career/success position goals.

Darlene Chadbourne

Chapter 9
Affirmations, Working Your Numbers

Affirmations are a wonderful tool using the vibration of words to get you opened up and plugged into the frequency that is yours to have and to hold. To acquire the freedom to live your own path and accomplish your mission in this lifetime.

When you can align yourself with the frequencies of your numerology blueprint, it is like using the right combination to easily open a safe. When you use affirmations to activate your personal number combinations, things open up for you; opportunities and synchronicities appear out of nowhere, or so it seems.

In reality, your higher self and guides are rejoicing that you are ready to get on your own unique path and start working toward your personal goals and mission for this lifetime. During this process you may encounter fear and resistance as the memories locked into your current life memory bank, your generational programming, or learned behavior come up. Past-life fears of being persecuted for the last time that you tried to accomplish your personal mission may surface. When those memories create resistance for you now, there are exercises and tools to use to move beyond these obstacles that might hold you back.

Who would think that you could find the freedom to change your vibration through numbers and the letters in the words we speak and the thoughts that we think every day? Pay attention to words that you use the most. Then figure out their numerical vibration or frequency to see if they are one of your blueprint numbers. Example: "I am receiving." Stated in this way, it means "I am receiving, for me, at this time." Specifically for me, Darlene, right now: "I am receiving the information I need to finish my book. Thank you and I am Grateful."

This is using the empowerment of your own "I AM" that you have uncovered in the process of doing numerology.

It may be difficult for you to do these affirmations and ask for the help you need because of situations where you have asked for help in the past but received things that hurt you, disempowered you, or suppressed you, to keep you trapped in the fear of receiving.

It is at those times that you might have put a lock on your heart and decided never to allow yourself to be vulnerable to receive that hurt or be put down again.

This is where affirmations applied on a daily basis either verbally or written, preferably both, over a period of time of anywhere from two weeks to a month, will help to open you up to change. As you get into the habit of doing this you will notice the time frame is much shorter.

I encourage you to attach words to the phrase "I AM" because it is a defining power statement in and of itself.

Darlene Chadbourne

As in the example "I AM receiving," it is stating "receiving" as if it is already happening. If you state, "I want to receive," you leave yourself open to always wanting to receive. "I am going to receive" puts it in the future and out of reach. Please be careful how you state things.

Numerology is a tool to use when you make the decision to step into your full passion, purpose, and potential, to find your "I AM" by *Naming, Claiming,* and *Becoming* the real, unique, free and fully empowered you.

The Poison of Criticism

Criticism is the enemy of the SELF.

Criticism causes you to retract the SELF.

Criticism makes you want to fortress and defend yourself.

Criticism causes temper tantrums.

Criticism teaches you to lash out and attack.

Criticism causes laziness—if you think you can't do it right, you won't do it at all.

Criticism makes you recoil all effort.

Criticism makes you think you are always wrong and never right.

Criticism gives power to others outside of the SELF.

Criticism leads to your own Criticism of the SELF.

Darlene Chadbourne, copyright 1998

(Criticism is a 13/4 energy, a number that means work and more work and no play.)

The Power of Words

If your letters in your name carry a vibration of energy, then each of the words we use will carry a vibration of a Universal number system energy or an energy signature. We use words to describe a thought in order to take action. Thanks to Louise Hay's book *Heal Your Body* for introducing me to the concept of affirmations. This had to do with changing an emotional belief that created a physical response. I have played with the concept of using affirmations to change living life in a habitual manner. Doing anything the same way I have always done it inevitably leads to being stagnant in the same place I have always been. So experiment with this, creating an affirmation and making the statement that works for you. I firmly believe that using multiple senses for acting out affirmations speed up the process of reprogramming the habitual belief.

The forms of transforming a belief are:

- Thinking it.
- Visualizing it.
- Hearing the sound of it, like hearing your full birth name said aloud.
- Writing it, the motion of forming each of the letters and acknowledging the vibrations by using hand/eye coordination.

I imagine our internal calculators computing the numerical vibration of each of the letters in a word.

I have had my clients use affirmations, with great success. Use "I AM" as the beginning of each statement.

"I AM" is a 14/5 vibration.

- 1 in the equation is about the self.
- 4 in the equation is about the material world of building.
- 5 in the equation is about being a free spirit and an agent of change.

I feel that when you want to create a change it is very good to start with "I AM."

An example might be, "I AM, therefore I Matter."

The numerical calculation for that statement is a 101/11/2.

The word Matter is a 14/5.

I have had clients experimenting with affirmations, with great results.

If you are looking for change, first find your "I AM" and then affirm what you choose to create in your life.

Which of the Blueprint positions would you like to focus on?

- Soul number representing the past.
- Personality number representing the present.
- Path of destiny number representing the future.

Darlene Chadbourne

- Inner guidance number representing the present and the future.
- Native path number representing the present and the lesson you are here to learn.
- Maturity number representing midlife years 35-65.
- Career success number representing the future.
- Fulfillment number representing the present, when you are fully satisfied.

Steps for Creating Affirmations

1. Find a word from the Wordlist, or a word that appears out of nowhere like mine did. Keep it personal to you. You can only create change in yourself. If it is another word that draws your attention, you now have the know-how to figure its numerical vibration. You can even add it to the list so you will have it for future use. If it is not from the list, you will need to use the letter chart to calculate the number vibration of the word. Then add together each of the numbers in the word to get a total and reduce it to a single digit.
2. Use the word you've chosen with the "I AM" or create your own statement that is short and sweet, direct and to the point of the change you want to create. To acquire the freedom you deserve. It is your "I AM" that allows you to Name "It", Claim "It", and Become "It". The "It" here is the freedom to be you.
3. Write your newly designed affirmation over and over again, filling a page or two. Do it before going to sleep at night and then place the page or the whole notebook under the pillow for your nightly re-programming session.
4. Say it often throughout the day. Sing it or chant it while you are driving alone in your car.
5. Post it around the house.

Darlene Chadbourne

6. Pay attention for signs in your everyday life. They may not be obvious right away or could be obvious immediately, depending on what they are. If nothing else they will be unusual enough, to get your attention.
7. Let go of all expectations of how it will manifest in your life. Know that it will, in ways that you least expect.

Darlene Chadbourne

(Apply the following to the Diagram on the opposite page.)

Above: Source, God, Universe are terms for the above.

    "A" Almighty, or All That Is energy.

Middle: You are the connecting rod joining the above and below at the Heart.

Below: Earth, your grounding place. Needed for physical manifestation.

    "M" Matter, Mother Earth, or Material World.

All three of these circles need to be equally connected to have the best experience here on earth. The word Roots is a 24/6 energy, and very fitting as the 6-pointed star or Merkaba that is overlaid on the "I AM" diagram.
"Merkaba means 'Chariot' in Hebrew" according to Tashira Tachi-ren in, *What is Lightbody?* p. 35.

So the Merkaba is your vehicle of choice for traversing through life. Once you make the connection of the above and below, become comfortably centered in who you are, rooted like the tree and able to pull the nutrients you need from the crystal core of the earth, and become firmly grounded, you can pull the nutrients up to the heart chakra. Then absorb and take them out to the very edges of the heavens, like the tree does pulling the heavenly energies down to the heart.

Darlene Chadbourne
~ 180 ~

Conclusion

Naming, Claiming, and Becoming your Full Purpose and Potential, of Empowerment, and Freedom.

If you don't feel that you are living your number's essence fully, empowering you to evolve beyond where you are, and to where you want to be, then it is time to determine what is in your way. It is time to go to the emotional release work. Words: Emotional Response = 80/8, abbreviated ER = 14/5

It is fitting that the "I AM" = 14/5 and the visual with Mantra can be traced with a number 8 energy.

When you have completed your number calculations and know your numbers that make up your blueprint, you have the tools to work with, to delve in and know yourself better. Now what do you do with this information?

You could be this, and you could be that. Are you living your numbers fully, empowering yourself to be all that you can be?

What is keeping you from realizing your freedom to be all that you can be? The emotional release process is where many of the answers lie. Emotional Responses to any and every scenario can be the reason for the sly, held back, and tethered energy that lurks in your background and memory bank of past events, whether it is in this life, or a past life. The soul's memory holds, as a reminder, past emotional responses that keep you in a safe place, for the time of the trauma. These emotional memories hold your power hostage and keep you in your place so you don't "get too big for your britches", or think you are better than anyone else.

    The emotional responses are safety valves that remind us of a previous time and what happened to get us in trouble, or punished, or hurt someone else. What if this happened at 5 years old when you were not mature enough to know the difference? What if you took full responsibility for something that happened back then that really had nothing to do with you? What if a sibling was always blaming you for something they did? What if you were the scapegoat and you have carried that energy forward with you for all these years? Thinking it was yours to own and be responsible for.

    All past scenarios can elicit an emotional response that lies in wait for the next chance that you have, to take your power back. Sometimes it slyly sneaks out and trips you up, once again disempowering you and keeping you stuck in an old emotional response that no longer serves you. Instead, it hurts your progress of evolution to move forward into the powerful person you are meant to be.

    Many times it is the emotional response hurdles that persist and prevent you from being all that you are meant to be in this lifetime.

    This is the time to use Part 2 of this book to open up through the tools provided, to reprogram your emotional response reactions into power statements, helping you to energize and activate your personal numbers into powerful emotional responses fueling your journey forward.

The old emotional responses keep you locked in a time capsule from your past. When you need to be so present in the *NOW* scenario, responding in a take-hold, take-charge movement that can fuel your future, *Name It*, *Claim It*, and *Become It*. This is the mentoring work that some choose after a full numerology reading.

The process requires you to give yourself permission to see clearly what hides behind your emotional response doors that is tripping you up every time you get to that empowering place to move forward. What is that emotional response that stops you in your tracks?

I have gotten to know this emotional response personally in getting this book written and completed. The emotional response came as many masks:

- "I am not good enough."
- "Who do you think you are?"
- "You can't write."
- "You have no imagination."
- "You aren't smart enough."

All of these old tapes hide slyly within you waiting for an opportunity to jump out in front of you on your path to empowerment, trying to keep you safe from making a mistake. This is your inner self-security that never wants you to take a risk and put yourself, your true self, out there to be all that you can be.

This is exactly what has held up the completion of this little self-help book that you are holding right now. So join me in reaching for your freedom from old emotional response prisons.

This is your old "boogie man" from the past that was lurking in the dark closet of your room. This is the closet with all the keys to your freedom through numbers. This is the breakthrough you have been waiting for to empower that freedom to be the truly powerful you.

This book is intended to give you the self-confidence you need to attain your freedom.

Darlene Chadbourne

Tools

Tool #1—Journaling

I strongly suggest you keep a daily entry journal, notating all of the unusual signs and clues that Spirit leaves for you on a daily basis. It could be a message on the radio or a license plate, a word or phrase, a line in a song or something someone says to you, or you overhear it in someone else's conversation. I usually perk up if I hear it two times in a short period of time, but if I hear it or see it three times or more, I feel it is time to take action.

Tool #2—Meditation

My favorite meditation with numbers and the "I AM" follows.
Go to http://www.sandrawalter.com/unity to find the mp3 meditation and access to the Global Meditations (the more hearts, the more impact!). Look for Christ Light Expansion on the website: http://www.sandrawalter.com/wp-content/uploads/2016/04/Christ-Light-Expansion.mp3

Here's a wonderful *Christ Light Activation* with beautiful visuals on YouTube: https://www.youtube.com/watch?v=Bqlsl30S1_U

Tool #3—Bubble-Up Exercise

Bubble-Up Exercise for Sensitivity

- Imagine blowing up bubble gum so big that you can walk into it and seal it up. This protects your aura.
- Write the affirmation below until you have it programmed enough to be able to say "Bubble up" when you go into an energy laden place.

" Only good and wonderful things come in—everything else bounces off with love."

Copyright 2000   Darlene Chadbourne

Tool #4—Releasing Karmic Connections

Letter to Dissolve Karma

Dear _____

I make amends for anything and everything in this lifetime and any previous lifetimes that I have done to hurt you or to disempower you.

I forgive you for anything and everything in this lifetime and any previous lifetimes that you have done to hurt me or to disempower me.

Copyright 2000   Darlene Chadbourne

Tool #5—Apply Shape and Form to your numbers and your "I AM" presence.

    Creating Your Sphere of Humanity

    Apply Merkaba to Sphere of Humanity

    Writing

    Journaling

Writing for your own purposes and processing or recording intuitive insights.

Tool #6—Mind-Mapping

This is a page of word-association starting with a word in the middle of the page. Then what does this word make you think of? Draw a line and place that word and any others words around the original word. You can also continue by doing the same with each of the words you added. If you write a sentence about each of the words when you are done you will have a few paragraphs all written.

Darlene Chadbourne

Appendix 1: Meaning or Qualities of the Numbers (quick reference)

Number Qualities

Number 1—leader, initiator, new ideas, head of the operation, stand out in front of the crowd, stay centered, allow the world to turn around you, release control, eliminate chaos, find peace and harmony in stillness, draw people and things to you.
Negative
Egotistic, selfish, greedy, tyrant, power over others, mean, oppressor, wants the spotlight on self, "me, myself, and I" attitude, and lack of consideration for others

Number 2— the power behind the throne, work well with others, peacemaker, conflict resolution, negotiator, politician, partner, base decisions on intuition, sensitive, chameleon, arbitrator, balancer, team player, stay in background, blend in, harmony at all costs, tendency to belittle self.
Negative
One-sided, either or thought process, create or stirs up conflict, argues over everything, dualistic, always negative, conflicted

Number 3—creator, communicator, performer, speaker, class clown, cheerleader, crafter, full of joy, happy-go-lucky, playful, easygoing, imaginative, self-expressive, creative clutter, talkative, artistic, love groups.

Negative

Scattered, flaky, flamboyant, demonstrative, lack of creativity, blah, heavy-hearted, moody

Number 4—To build and manifest in the material world, solid, secure, foundation, square, four corners, cornerstone, cross-roads, organized, stabilized, work, contains, limiting.

Negative

Workaholic, rigid, stubborn, bearing a cross, burdened, heavy, stuck, martyr

Number 5—Free spirit, sensitive, sexual, sensual, guide for wisdom, teacher, salesperson, traveler, language, written word, media, advertising, adaptable, a channel, liberation, limitless, possibilities, free of attachment to outcome, school, awareness through the five senses,

Negative

Oppression, false images, setbacks, disappointment, additions, lack of grounding

Number 6—Harmony, balance, horizon, beauty, male/female, family, children, health, healing, landscape, interior design, visual, music, art, sunrise/sunset, equality, love, balancing duality, being fair

Negative

Judgmental, possessive, nosy, one-sided, unbalanced, narcissistic

Number 7—Quiet, presence, studious, contemplative, deep thought, philosophy, curiosity, teacher/student, studies, education, retreat, meditation, monk, nun, priest, priestess, faith, belief, mystical, peace, tranquility.

Negative

Recluse, busy bee

Number 8—Flow, trust, above and below, working together, business, finances, self-employed, multitasking, in unison, wealth, money, management, consciousness, abundance, balance, achieve.

Negative

Stagnant, loss, poverty, conflict with others, judgmental, criticism

Number 9—Completion, love, artist, humanitarian, spiritual, compassionate, vulnerable, sensitive, feeling, unconditional love, service

Negative

Vulnerable, fear of abandonment, stubborn, drama king or queen, nosy, hold grudge, can't let go

Number 0—Nothing and everything, god, universe, spirit, enhances and uplifts.

No Negative for 0

Appendix 2: Blueprint

Numerology Blueprint

```
1 2 3 4 5 6 7 8 9
A B C D E F G H I
J K L M N O P Q R
S T U V W X Y Z
1 2 3 4 5 6 7 8 9
```

SOUL	#

Full Name at Birth:

PERSONALITY	#
PATH OF DESTINY	#
INNER GUIDANCE	#

Date of Birth:

NATIVE PATH	#
MATURITY PATH	#
CAREER/SUCCESS	#
FULFILLMENT	#

Personal Epicycle (Month + Day + Current Year):

Last Birthday:

PERSONAL YEAR	2020#
Jan to Jan	2021#

See p. 125 for information on how to do the Personal Year.

Freedom Through Numbers
~ 193 ~

Appendix 3: Star Templates

6-POINT STAR POWER

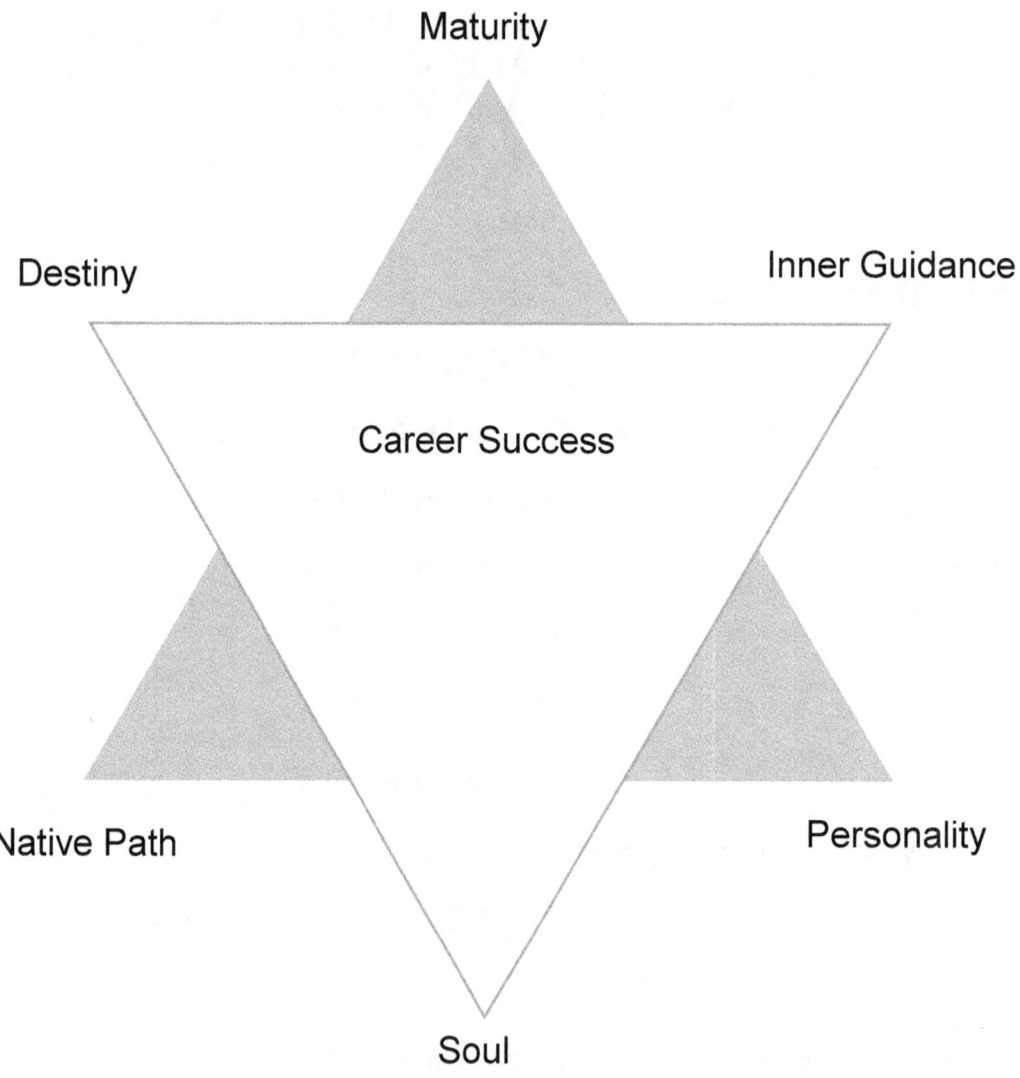

Darlene Chadbourne

3D SIX-POINT STAR POWER

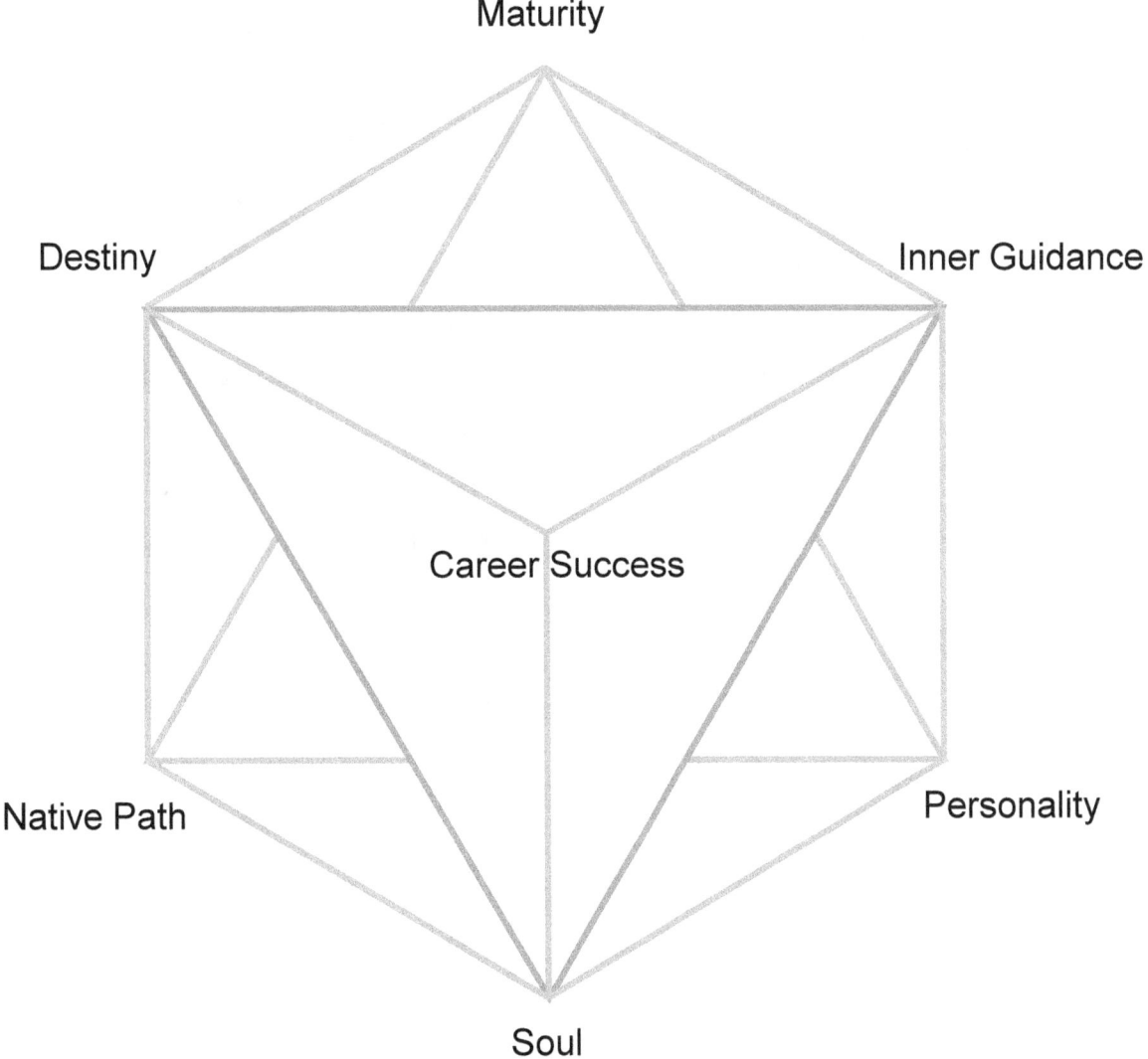

Freedom Through Numbers

Appendix 4: Word Lists for Creating Affirmations

Vibration of words or phrases and their numbers

10/1	19/10/1	28/10/1	37/10/1	46/10/1
Fast	Sexual	Being	Ambitious	Charming
	Sexy	Content	Assertive	Exciting
		Focused	Bright	Listening
		Elegant	Conscious	Persistent
			Expanded	Pro-active
			Female	Wonderful
			Limitless	
			Motivated	
			Perfect	
			Radiance	
			Reliable	
			Sincere	
			Worthy	
			Vitality	

55/10/1	64/10/1	73/10/1	82/10/1	91/10/1
Intelligent	True Humility	Part of the Whole		

Darlene Chadbourne

11/2	20/2	29/11/2	38/11/2	47/11/2
Calm	Valued	Adored	Authentic	Comfortable
Kind	Wise	Clever	Available	Mysterious
		Mobile	Centered	Mystified
		Plenty	Connected	Particular
		Proud	Creative	Training
		Rich	Discreet	
			Exuberant	
			Passionate	
			Practical	
			Reasonable	
			Satisfied	
			Smiling	
			Successful	

56/11/2	65/11/2	74/11/2	83/11/2	92/11/2
Independent	Hard-working	Self-disciplined		Spiritually connected
Imaginative	Self-empowered			

101/11/2

Taking responsibility

Freedom Through Numbers

12/3	21/3	30/3	39/12/3	48/12/3
	Aware	Happy	Competent	Diplomatic
	Brave	Genius	Consistent	Easygoing
	Clear	Playful	Desirable	Friendly
	Famous	Sociable	Diligent	Intuitive
	Noble	Strong	Flexible	Inventive
	Useful	Wisely	Satisfied	Thoughtful
	Visual		Submissive	
			Versatile	In my life
			Wholeness	

57/12/3	66/12/3	75/12/3	84/12/3	93/12/3
Cooperative		Experiencing		Creating new thoughts
Discerning				The power of choice
Exhilarated				
Gregarious				
Perceptive				
Good enough				

Darlene Chadbourne
~ 198 ~

13/4	22/4	31/4	40/4	49/13/4
Neat	Alive	Father	Focusing	Deserving
Safe	Capable	Fearless	Humorous	Enthusiastic
Male	Cleaning out	Patient	Innocent	Inspired
	Fearless	Sensible	Involved	Integrated
	Funny	Welcomed	Liberated	Original
	Ideal		Sufficient	Receptive
	Integrative			Sympathetic
	Loved			
	Master			
	Modest			
	Nice			
	Tidy			
	Valuable			
	Wanted			

58/13/4	67/13/4	76/13/4	85/13/4	94/13/4
Perception	Pioneering			Part of a higher plan
Grown up now				

14/5	23/5	32/5	41/5	50/5
I am	Abundant	Direct	Attracting	Efficient
Key	Good	Guided	Creating	Empowered
Joy	Matter	In Love	Flowing	Energetic
	Open	Logical	Fruitful	Infinite
	Sacred	Polite	Generous	Purposeful
		Power	Heartfelt	
		Willful	Holistic	
			I am that I am	
			Powerful	
			Radiance	
			Remarkable	
			Respected	
			Sensitive	
			Unified	
			Willing	

59/14/5	68/14/5	77/14/5	86/14/5	95/14/5
Disciplined	Clear-thinking		A powerful creator	Accessing the Divine
Interesting	A precious Gift			
Professional	Created for love			

15/6	24/6	33/6	42/6	51/6
Self	Active	Fulfilled	Accepting	Compassionate
	Artist	Initiate	Compassionate	Completing
	Great	Relaxed	Different	Self-confident
	Jovial		Miraculous	Understanding
	Lovable		Spontaneous	
	Merkaba			
	Pure			

60/6	69/15/6	78/15/6	87/15/6
Worthwhile	More out-going	Accessing my power	
Loving Myself		Willing to change	

96/15/6

Feeling full & complete

Freedom Through Numbers
~ 201 ~

16/7	25/7	34/7	43/7	52/7
One	Free	Beautiful	Adventurous	Cherished
Okay	Humble	Certain	Brilliant	Determined
	Pleasant	Complete	Coherent	Expressive
	Quick	Complex	Grounded	Harmonious
	Witty	Curious	Honored	Optimistic
		Enough	Positive	Prolific
		Excited	Protected	Transformed
	a Magnet	Healthy	Unlimited	Victorious
		Loving	Wholesome	
		Mindful	Working	
		Mother		
		Noticed		
		Present		
		Romantic		
		Seeking		

61/7	70/7	79/16/7	88/16/7	97/16/7
Integrating		Straightforward		Divinely empowered

Darlene Chadbourne

17/8	26/8	35/8	44/8			
Clean	Adaptable	Amazing	Achiever			
Fit	Funny	Complete	Courageous			
	Healed	Daring	Intellectual			
	Joyful	Distinct	Powerful			
	Ready	Grateful	Quick-witted			
	Secure	Helpful	Respectful			
	Tough	Moving	Spiritual			
		Prompt	Supported			
			Unlimited			

53/8	62/8	71/8	80/8	89/17/8	98/17/8
Appreciated	The Authority	Comprehensive	Uncompromising		
Approachable		Philosophical			
Broad-minded		Surrendering			Divinely protected
Deeply loved					Full of Intelligence
Processing					
Resourceful					
Responsible					
Thriving					

Freedom Through Numbers

18/9	27/9	36/9	45/9
Love	Accurate	Balancing	Confident
Lucky	Gentle	Divine	Congruent
	Heard	Grateful	Effective
	Honest	Popular	Embracing
	Leader	Rational	Important
	Quiet	Starting	Methodical
	Whole		Releasing

54/9	63/9	72/9	81/9	90/9	99/18/9
Accomplished	Appropriate			On a positive mission	
Androgynous	Lighthearted				
an Illuminator					
Impressive					
Incredible					
Invincible					
Prosperous					
Warmhearted					

Darlene Chadbourne
~ 204 ~

The Merkeba

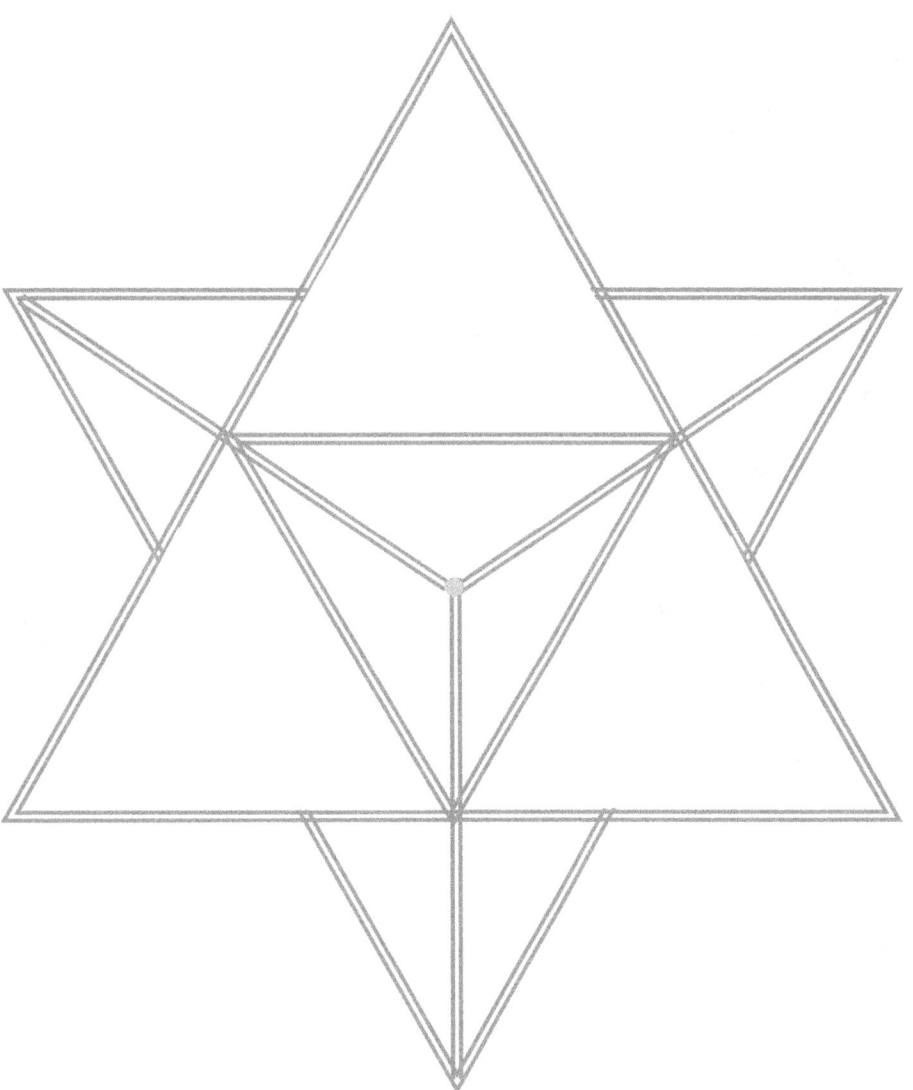

Freedom Through Numbers
~ 205 ~

Suggested Reading List

Numerology and the Divine Triangle
    Faith Javane and Dusty Bunker

The Complete Book of Numbers
    Steven Scott Pither

Cutting the Ties that Bind
    Phyllis Krystal

The Circle of Stones and *I Sit Listening to the Wind*
    Judith Duerk

The Dance of Deception
    Harriet Lerner

The Pythagorean Sourcebook and Library
    Guthrie & Fideler

The Master Numbers in Numerology
    Korra Deaver

Way of the Great Oracle, The Voyager Tarot
    James Wanless

What is Lightbody?
    Tashira Tachi-ren

Darlene Chadbourne

Acknowledgements

Thank you with all of my heart to my children Jodie, Jim, Jason, and Jeff for surviving my vacant-mom syndrome through your younger years and turning out to be the wonderful people that you are today. You have all helped me to get to this point.

My deepest appreciation goes to my loving companion Hank for giving me the time, space, and encouragement to complete this midlife dream.

Many thanks to my college friends, Carol, Mary, and Susan for the continuous encouragement to keep writing, and to Martha VanderWolk for her wonderful guidance and inspiration.

I'm also very grateful to all of the human angels in my life—Becky, Ed, Hank, Kenn, Rebecca, and Sandy—who have shored me up and kept me going in so many supportive ways.

To my special tech angels, Jodie, Katherine, Nicole, and Norman: without you, this book would still be a stack of printed paper sitting on my desk forever weighed down by my dream of publishing it.

I also offer my thanks to all of the incredible angels who took the time to read and edit this book: Mary, Brie, Carol, Hank, Karen, Jodie, Nicole, and Norman.

An especially big thank you for being guided to Katherine Mayfield's lecture on self-publishing. She has been an incredible finishing editor and has helped to get this manuscript in the format that is needed for our new modern publishing world. She has worn many hats for me, from computer graphics and visuals, to seasoned advice of what she has found that works best.

In the graphics department, Nicole has worked with me from the beginning, helping me take my thoughts and ideas and putting them into the original PowerPoint. That was the very first step to this book coming into being. Then she bailed me out with typical last-minute changes.

Jodie has hosted many of my graphics, websites, computer-and-shoulder-to-cry-on moments, and has contributed to this book every step of the way. Norman has kept my computer in tip-top shape.

Thanks to my photographers, Megan and Jimm, who have captured my spirit with their photographic expertise.

I offer special thanks to my writer's retreat leader Lynne Klippel and companion writers Jimm, Sally, Joan, Natasha, Peggy Lee, Kathy, and Kathleen.

Then there is the wonderful astrologer, author, and friend Dusty Bunker, whom Spirit nicely put right before my eyes many times along the way. She has had gigantic confidence in my work with clients and in my ability to get this book done. She has guided me in so many ways. She was my beginning point.

Darlene Chadbourne

And finally, many thanks to my go-to gurus, who have brought me through thick and thin: Ann Marie, Betsey, Chris, Donna, Dorothy, Ginger, Gloria, Jan, Julie, Kathy, Laurra, MaryAnn, MaryLiz, Marsha, Mindy, Padi, Patrick, Stacy, and Robert.

My heartfelt gratitude also goes to my traveling companions Hank, Becky, Ed, Kathy, Julie, and Chris, who helped me cross the deep chasm between grief and happiness.

About the Author

Darlene Chadbourne is a Master Numerologist who lives in Maine. She uses numerology as a basis for mentoring men and women through changes according to the original passions and purpose that they entered this life to accomplish. She empowers people to know who they have the potential to be through their personal numbers.

Darlene has worked with clients for nearly 30 years, from newborns to those in their eighties, both nationally and internationally, by phone, computer, and in person. She has been interviewed on the radio, spoken at many events, and written magazine articles. She loves to teach classes and speak to groups. Give her an audience, and her passion for what she does comes alive and is amplified.

She graduated from Norwich University with a degree in Psychology and Holistic Studies in her fifties.

www.ingramcontent.com/pod-product-compliance
Lightning Source LLC
Chambersburg PA
CBHW081153290426
44108CB00018B/2536